Leveraged ESOPs and Employee Buyouts

Fifth Edition

Leveraged ESOPs and Employee Buyouts

Fifth Edition

Edited by Scott S. Rodrick

The National Center for Employee Ownership (NCEO)
Oakland, California

This publication is designed to provide accurate and authoritative information regarding the subject matter covered. It is sold with the understanding that the publisher is not engaged in rendering legal, accounting, or other professional services. If legal advice or other expert assistance is required, the services of competent professionals should be sought.

Legal, accounting, and other rules affecting business often change. Before making decisions based on the information you find here or in any publication from any publisher, you should ascertain what changes might have occurred and what changes might be forthcoming. The NCEO's Web site (including the members-only area) and newsletter for members provide regular updates on these changes. If you have any questions or concerns about a particular issue, check with your professional advisor or, if you are an NCEO member, call or email us.

Leveraged ESOPs and Employee Buyouts, 5th ed.
Editing and book design by Scott S. Rodrick

© 2005 by The National Center for Employee Ownership. All rights reserved. Published 2005.

First edition 1997. Second edition 1999. Third edition 2000. Fourth edition 2001. Fifth edition 2005, reprinted with corrections 2009.

Printed in the United States of America.

ISBN: 1-932924-02-7

No part of this book may be reproduced or transmitted in any form or by any means, electronic or mechanical, including photocopying, recording, or by any information storage and retrieval system, without prior written permission from the publisher.

The National Center for Employee Ownership
1736 Franklin St., 8th Flr.
Oakland, CA 94612
(510) 208-1300
(510) 272-9510 (fax)
Email: *nceo@nceo.org*
Web site: *http://www.nceo.org/*

Contents

	Preface	vii
1.	**A Primer on Leveraged ESOPs** *Corey Rosen*	1
2.	**Contribution and Allocation Limits for Leveraged ESOPs** *Luis Granados*	25
3.	**Section 1042 and the Tax-Deferred ESOP "Rollover"** *Scott S. Rodrick*	41
4.	**Financing the Leveraged ESOP** *Kenneth E. Serwinski*	57
5.	**Senior Credit Underwriting for ESOP Transactions** *Mary Sullivan Josephs*	65
6.	**Valuation Issues in Leveraged ESOPs** *Richard C. May, Robert L. McDonald, and David C. Light*	111
7.	**Accounting for Employee Stock Ownership Plan Transactions** *Rebecca J. Miller*	129
8.	**The Feasibility Study for the Employee-Led Buyout** *Deborah Groban Olson*	159
9.	**ESOPs in Mergers and Acquisitions** *Laurence A. Goldberg*	195
	About the Authors	207
	About the NCEO	211

Preface

During the past few decades, employee stock ownership plans (ESOPs) have become a familiar feature on the U.S. business landscape. Here at the National Center for Employee Ownership (NCEO), we estimate there are currently over 11,000 companies with ESOPs, covering roughly 8.5 million participants. Many of these ESOPs are leveraged, meaning that the ESOP has borrowed money on the credit of the employer or other related parties to buy company stock. It is the only qualified employee benefit plan that can do this. Moreover, the company can deduct ESOP contributions it makes for both principal and interest payments on the loan. This tax-advantaged leveraging capability makes the ESOP an ideal vehicle for several purposes:

- To sell part or all of a company to its employees. This is a popular use in closely held companies, where the ESOP provides a market for the stock of the selling owner. If the company is a C corporation and the ESOP owns 30% of more of the company after the sale, the owner can postpone or avoid taxation of the sale proceeds by using the tax-deferred "rollover" under Section 1042 of the Internal Revenue Code. The buyout can proceed in stages, e.g., a leveraged buyout of 50% of the company repaid over seven years, followed by another leveraged transaction for the remainder.
- To divest a subsidiary, division, or product line through an ESOP buyout. Note that whether the buyout is of a company or a part thereof, outside investors may participate in the transaction.
- To enable public companies to repurchase shares from the market using pretax dollars. (At times, this has been used as a takeover defense.)
- To restructure existing benefit plans by replacing them with an ESOP.

- To acquire capital by having the company borrow through the ESOP and repay the loan with pretax dollars. Here, the ESOP takes out a loan to buy newly issued company stock. The company (which now has the ESOP's loan proceeds as payment for the stock) repays the loan with pretax dollars and deducts the contributions. In this way the company obtains a low-cost loan, although the newly issued shares dilute the non-ESOP shareholders' ownership interest.

ESOPs are complicated mechanisms, and using leverage increases the complexity. This book is designed to be a practical tool for anyone dealing with that complexity, whether the leveraged ESOP will purchase a small amount of stock or be used for an employee buyout of part or all of a company. Beginning with "A Primer on Leveraged ESOPs," the book then moves on to cover contribution and allocation limits (chapter 2), the Section 1042 tax-deferred "rollover" (chapter 3), financing (chapters 4 and 5), valuation (chapter 6), accounting (chapter 7), employee buyout feasibility studies (chapter 8), and mergers and acquisitions (chapter 9).

Much of the material here first appeared in the NCEO's *Journal of Employee Ownership Law and Finance,* which is the only professional journal in the U.S. focusing solely on ESOPs and equity compensation. The *Journal,* which appears quarterly, features a variety of articles written by experts and submitted to blind review by an editorial board comprised of prominent practitioners and academics. All the previously published material in this book has been revised and updated where necessary to reflect changes in the law.

We hope that you find this book informative and helpful and that it inspires you to consider whether a leveraged ESOP is right for your company. For further information, see the NCEO's other publications on ESOPs, employee ownership, and employee participation; attend our events devoted to these matters; consult our Web site at *http://www.nceo.org/;* and, if you are not already a member of the NCEO, join and use us as a resource.

Fifth Edition (2005)

With the fifth edition, various chapters have been updated, and the book as a whole as been streamlined, with unnecessary material removed and other material added.

Chapter 1

A Primer on Leveraged ESOPs

Corey Rosen

If you already have wealth, it's not so hard to raise more of it by borrowing money. Firms like KKR, The Carlyle Group, Hicks Muse, and other buyout funds can borrow billions to buy target companies. The theory is that the companies they buy will earn enough profit to repay the loans, so the acquisition becomes self-liquidating. Wealth builds more wealth. But what if you aren't a wealthy investment group but rather just a bunch of ordinary employees who want to become owners of their own companies? Like the investment group, you'll want to borrow money to buy an investment that you believe will be profitable enough to pay back the loan. But unlike the investment firm, you'll actually work there and watch over that investment with extra care. Your group might have a great business plan, a reasonable price for the assets, and the support of existing management, but unless you have some pretty solid collateral, you don't have a chance. Unless, that is, you can borrow money through an employee stock ownership plan (ESOP). Established by federal law in 1974 as part of the Employee Retirement Income Security Act (ERISA), ESOPs were specifically created to make it possible for ordinary employees to borrow money to buy stock in their companies.

In fact, employees have borrowed over $400 billion to buy stock in their own companies since 1974. At least 4,000 companies are now majority-owned through an ESOP, and thousands more partially owned. How can health care assistants, bank tellers, and machine operators use ESOPs to borrow that much money? Have the homes, cars, and firstborn of American employees been heedlessly pledged as collateral to allow everyday workers to become big-time wheeler-dealers?

Not at all. The simple idea behind ESOPs is that if Congress provided tax incentives to owners of existing businesses to provide collateral to back up ESOP loans, at least some business owners would be tempted. The ESOP could then use that collateral to obtain the funding to buy shares from the company or the owners. The company would repay the loan out of its future earnings, earnings the employees would help create.

Congress gave companies a variety of tax incentives to use ESOPs as a means of acquiring company shares. ESOPs could do all sorts of things. They could buy out retiring owners of privately held companies; they could finance capital growth at lower after-tax costs; and they could buy back existing shares and pay for them, in part, out of the tax-deductible earnings of those very shares.

In return for this largess, Congress insisted on some rules. "ESOPs must be fair," Congress decreed, and proceeded to write pages of laws, which led to chapters of regulations, which led to volumes of interpretations and commentaries on just what "fair" means. What follows here is an introduction to all these benefits and rules. Complex as they can be, however, the core concept is simple: ESOPs are a way to use the future earnings of the corporation to acquire ownership for employees. Tax benefits and, hopefully, the employees themselves help provide the added economic value to generate these additional earnings. In return for the tax benefits, companies must comply with rules designed to make sure the plans are rigorous enough to really provide benefits to employees, but not so rigorous that no company would set them up. The complexity of the laws is something that can easily be handled by professional advisors; people in companies just need to know the essential outlines.

What Is an ESOP?

An ESOP is a kind of employee benefit plan. Governed by ERISA (the Employee Retirement Income Security Act), ESOPs were given a specific statutory framework in 1974 and were the subject of new legislation, mostly to add benefits, in almost every Congress between 1974 and 1986. Like other tax-qualified deferred compensation plans under Section 401(a) of the Internal Revenue Code (the "Code"), such as profit sharing plans and pensions, ESOPs must be operated for "the exclusive benefit of plan participants." This does not mean exactly what it says, though. It does not mean that other people cannot benefit from ESOPs, because no one would set them up were that the case. It does mean that when the interests of the participants of the plan conflict with the interests of people outside the plan, the participants should win. Moreover, ESOPs must be operated by a trustee in a manner that is prudent and in compliance with the fiduciary rules of ERISA. Buying stock in the ESOP's sponsor when you, as trustee, know the company is about to encounter severe problems, for instance, is not prudent. Finally, ESOPs, like other qualified deferred compensation plans, must not discriminate in their operations in favor of highly compensated employees, officers, and owners. As was said of the Golden Rule, "all the rest is commentary."

Technically, an ESOP is a stock bonus plan qualified to borrow money. Whereas stock bonus plans are only required to distribute their benefits in the form of employer securities but can hold any mix of investments they like while people are still in the plan, ESOPs are required to invest primarily in employer stock. While there is no regulation about what "primarily" means, most ESOP specialists think it is over 50%. The percentage probably can temporarily drop below that from time to time, perhaps even for a year or two, and the rest of the assets can be invested in any sound investments. ESOPs can also start off by just receiving cash contributions from the company that are intended to buy stock later. Again, there is no consensus on how long an ESOP can do this, but doing it for two or three years seems safe. This "primarily invested" rule does not relieve the trustee of the duty to be prudent and comply with ERISA's fiduciary rules, but it helps. Investing primarily in an employer's stock can be unwise for a profit sharing plan, and illegal for a pension plan (pension plans can only invest 10% of their assets in employer stock), but it is the law for ESOPs. Trustees, however, must take care that any particular decision to buy, hold, or sell stock in an ESOP makes sense for the plan participants.

How Leveraged ESOPs Work

Essentially, a leveraged ESOP is an intermediary in a loan transaction. Rather than borrow the money directly, a company borrows money and reloans it to an ESOP.

The company first sets up a employee stock ownership trust. The trust then borrows money to acquire stock in the company. The stock can be shares already owned, treasury shares, or new shares issued specifically for sale to the ESOP. Proceeds from the loan can be used for any legitimate business purpose. The stock is put into a "suspense account," where it is released to employee accounts as the loan is repaid. After employees leave the company or retire, the company pays them the stock purchased on their behalf. In the typical ESOP transaction, the lender will loan to the company, which reloans the money to the ESOP. Provided certain rules are followed, this "inside" loan does not have to be on the same terms as the "outside" loan, although it often is. Lenders prefer loaning directly to the company, but the accounting and tax effects of this two-step process are essentially the same as if the loan were made directly to the ESOP.

In return for agreeing to borrow through the ESOP, the company receives significant tax benefits, provided it follows the rules to assure employees are treated fairly. First, the company can deduct the entire loan contribution it makes to the ESOP, within certain payroll-based limits described below. That means the company, in effect, can deduct interest and principal on the loan, not just interest. Second, the company, if a C corporation, can deduct dividends paid on the shares acquired with the proceeds of the loan that are used to repay the loan itself (in other words, the earnings of the stock being acquired help pay for stock itself). Again, there are limits, as described below in sections on the rules of the loan and contribution limits.

Uses of Leveraged ESOPs

An ESOP can borrow money for any business purpose. The most common of these is to buy out shares of an existing owner in a closely held C corporation. Under Section 1042 of the Code, a company can set up an ESOP and have it borrow money to buy shares from an existing owner. If the ESOP owns at least 30% of the shares in the company after that transaction, that sale, plus any subsequent sales, qualifies the seller to reinvest the proceeds in securities of U.S. operating companies and defer tax on the gain made from the sale to the ESOP until these replacement investments are sold. This tax benefit applies only to closely held C corporations; the seller must be an individual, an estate, one of certain trusts, a partnership, or an S corporation. Shares must have been held for at least three years (if the ownership form changes, such as from a partnership to an S corporation, the ownership of the shares in the new entity "tacks" onto the shares of the old one).

While this is the most common application of a leveraged ESOP, it is only one of several potential uses. For instance, an ESOP can be used to buy another company, an increasingly common application. Because contributions to the ESOP to repay the loan are tax-deductible, the acquisition can be made in pretax dollars. In this application, a company can, for instance, print new shares or issue treasury shares to sell to an ESOP, which borrows money to acquire them. Then the company uses the loan proceeds to purchase the target and repays the loan with tax-deductible contributions to the ESOP. Alternatively, the acquiring company could do a tax-free stock-for-stock merger with the target. Then the ESOP could borrow money to buy out the shares (now shares of the acquiring company) from the owners of the target. If both companies are closely held C corporations, as explained in the chapter on mergers and acquisitions, it is possible to structure this transaction so that if it meets the rules for the tax-deferred rollover described above, the seller or sellers can qualify for a tax deferral of gains on the sale.

Another application for a leveraged ESOP is to acquire new capital. Any ESOP, whether in a C or S corporation, or a public or closely held corporation, can use an ESOP this way. Here, the company issues new shares or treasury shares and sells them to the ESOP, which borrows the funds to acquire the stock. The sale proceeds then are used to acquire new machinery, buildings, inventory, or any other property that might otherwise be financed. The company can then repay the loan through the ESOP in pretax dollars. Of course, this will have the impact of diluting other shareholders, but it also provides an employee benefit at the same time it is financing growth more efficiently. A similar approach can be used to refinance debt. Public companies also use leveraged ESOPs to buy back shares from the market.

ESOPs are also commonly used in divestitures of subsidiaries. Here, a new acquisition corporation is established. It sets up an ESOP for the employees of the entity being sold. The acquisition company ("Newco") then borrows money, which it reloans to the ESOP, to enable the ESOP to buy newly issued shares in Newco. Newco uses the money from the sale to buy assets for the parent and then repays the ESOP loan out of future revenues.

In all these transactions, it is possible and sometimes necessary to combine the ESOP purchase with equity investments from managers, outsiders, or even the employees themselves. These investments do not count as ESOP ownership, however, when calculating tax benefits. For instance, if an ESOP buys 30% of a company and managers 20%, the seller in a C corporation can defer taxes only of the sale of the 30% to the ESOP.

Finally, leveraged ESOPs are often done in stages so that the company does not have the burden of repaying excessive debt all at once.

Setting Up a Leveraged ESOP

The Trust

Setting up a leveraged ESOP raises several issues. First, what is a trust? Generally speaking, a trust is an arrangement whereby property is transferred to a "trustee" who administers it for the benefit of a designated beneficiary. In particular, an ESOP trust is a legal entity that holds property, mainly company stock contributed by the employer or bought with funds contributed by the employer, for the ESOP's participants. Like other trusts, the ESOP trust is designed to protect its beneficiaries. A trustee is appointed to do this. The ESOP trustee must ensure that the shares are valued properly, must vote the shares (although at whose direction is an issue to which we will return), must ensure that employee accounts are properly maintained, and must otherwise attend to the rules of ESOPs.

To help assure independence, many ESOP companies appoint bank trust departments or other trust companies to serve this function. Other companies appoint managers or other insiders as trustees. The law does not prohibit insiders from acting as trustees, despite their potential conflict of interest. If a conflict should arise, however, and the ESOP, the company's board, and other at-risk parties are brought to court, the presence of an independent trustee may weigh in the company's favor.

Who Can Be Lenders

Just about anyone can lend the ESOP money, including commercial lenders, sellers, and the company itself. ESOPs can also issue bonds to raise money, although this has been rare in recent years and is limited to the largest transactions. When a "party-in-interest" such as the seller or the company makes a loan, the terms of the loan must be not less favorable than an arm's length transaction (that is, similar to what might be available from a commercial lender).

When a seller lends to an ESOP, this can be in an installment sale. If the company is a C corporation and the ESOP ends up with at least 30% of the company's stock, the seller can still qualify for one of the main benefits of an ESOP, the ability to defer taxation on gains made from the sale by reinvesting in qualified replacement investments. Only amounts reinvested during the period from 3 months before to 12 months after the sale qualify, however. The sellers cannot simply keep reinvesting and rolling over their installment payments. The seller can reinvest an amount up to the entire value of the sale, however, by using other funds. One popular approach addresses this problem by allowing sellers to buy long-term bonds with the loan proceeds. A broker would sell bonds equal in value to the note; the seller would use the first installment of the note as a down payment and borrow the rest from a bank using the bond as collateral.

How the Money Is Borrowed

Most ESOP loan diagrams show the ESOP borrowing the money directly, then using it to buy company shares. The company then makes contributions to the ESOP to repay the loan. The ESOP may pledge the stock as collateral, but the company almost always must guarantee the loan with something more persuasive (assets or earnings). In addition, in many cases where the seller is reinvesting in qualified replacement property, the lender asks for part or all of these securities as collateral. Generally, as the loan is repaid, that portion of the collateral is released.

In practice, most loans are actually made to the company, which relends the money to the ESOP on the same or similar terms. Most lenders prefer to lend to the company. That way, they have better access to collateral and the company's cash flow, and fewer potential legal conflicts. The company can, however, make its loan to the ESOP on different terms than its loan from the lender, provided the transaction is an arm's length equivalent and the new terms of the loan to the ESOP meet fiduciary concerns (this is described in more detail below).

What Company Stock Can Be Used

ESOP rules are very strict on what qualifies as company stock. In closely held companies, the ESOP loan can only acquire stock with the highest combination of voting and dividend rights, or preferred stock readily convertible into such stock. In practice, that means ESOPs acquire either voting common stock or convertible preferred stock. In public companies, the ESOP can acquire any kind of common stock that is publicly traded. While the shares almost always must be voting shares, who votes them and how is more complex than it seems (it is not necessarily the employees). This is discussed in detail below.

In using preferred shares, it is important to make sure that the capitalization structure is not unfavorable to employee interests. Preferred shares whose upside potential is capped in value, for instance, are not considered in the employees' best interest. Preferred stock also must be structured carefully to assure that the conversion premium (the difference between the price of the preferred and the price of the common) is reasonable at the time the shares are issued.

Some companies have faced a problem when they issue dividend-paying stock to employees and find that under state laws they must pay the same dividends to holders of this stock outside the plan. This problem can be remedied, however, by changing the non-ESOP shares into some kind of non-dividend paying security beforehand.

The Rules of the Loan

A loan to an ESOP must meet several requirements. The loan must be at a reasonable interest rate, and only the stock in the ESOP acquired with the proceeds of the loan can be used as collateral (although the company or seller can, and almost invariably does, make its own guarantee with the lender). Only the dividends of the shares in the plan, contributions from the employer to repay the loan, and earnings from other investments in the trust contributed by the employer can be used to repay the loan. This means that dividends paid on shares acquired by the ESOP outside of the loan cannot be used to repay the loan, nor can the ESOP normally sell off shares in the trust to repay the loan unless the plan is terminated or the company is sold. In that case, all unpaid-for shares can be sold to repay the loan, with any amounts remaining after the sale being allocated to employees.

The loan must be without recourse to the ESOP, and must be for a specified term. The interest rate can be variable or fixed. There is no limit on the term of the loan to the company other than what lenders will accept (normally 5 to 10 years). Because the loan is usually made to the company and then reloaned to the ESOP, however, these bank-imposed limits do not necessarily limit the term of the company-to-ESOP loan. Provided the company can show that extending the term benefits employees, the term of the company-to-ESOP loan can be longer. For instance, extending the term of the loan to fit within the annual contribution limits would clearly benefit employees because, without such an extension, the plan would be disqualified. Extending the term to keep benefit levels more constant over a longer term might also qualify provided the benefit levels are significant.

Shares in the plan must be held in a suspense account. As the loan is repaid, these shares are released to the accounts of plan participants. The release must follow one of two formulas. The simplest is that the percentage of shares released equals the percentage of principal paid, either that year or during whatever shorter repayment period is used. In these cases, however, the release cannot be slower than what normal amortization schedules would provide for a 10-year loan with level payments of principal and interest. The principal-only method usually has the effect of releasing fewer shares to participants in the early years.

Alternatively, the company can release shares based on the percentage remaining in the account based on principal and interest paid. To do this the company divides the principal and interest payment it makes by the sum of (1) the principal and interest it still needs to pay and (2) the principal and interest it paid already that year. Stated more simply, the company bases its release on the total amount of principal and interest it pays rather than on the amount of the principal it repays. ESOP loans with a term of over 10 years must use this principal-plus-interest approach.

In either case, it is important to remember that the dollar value of the shares released each year is rarely the same as the amount contributed to repay the loan. If the price of the shares goes up, the amount allocated will be higher, in dollar terms, than the amount contributed; if they go down, the dollar value of the amount released will be lower. The amount *contributed to repay principal* is what counts for determining whether the company is within the limits for contributions allowed each year.

Refinancing ESOP Loans

Companies can refinance an existing non-ESOP loan with an ESOP loan under the same rules as if the loan were a new one. If a loan is refinanced, the shares are still allocated based on their original purchase price. Companies can refinance a loan that is reloaned to an ESOP without restriction because that transaction is between the company and the lender. ESOP loans themselves can also be refinanced under limited circumstances. Generally, a company wants to extend the existing term of the loan. In some cases, this is done because the company's payroll has shrunk, and the existing term requires payments that are above the contribution limits. In other cases, the company needs to repay the loan more slowly because of cash flow problems. The Department of Labor (DOL) has approved such refinancings. However, some companies want to refinance because their stock value has risen quickly, and they believe they are delivering "too much" value to employees. The DOL is much less favorable toward these refinancings.

Buying Back Unallocated Shares

Shares that have not yet been paid for are held in suspense before being allocated when loan payments are made. Some companies want to buy these shares back from the ESOP, often because they see them as a good value or because managers want to own more shares. In general, regulatory bodies frown on this because it denies employees an implied future benefit. Such repurchases are approved only in unusual circumstances. Note that this scenario is different from an outside purchase of all ESOP shares. That can be done if the ESOP trustee deems the sale to be in the best interests of plan participants.

Limitations on Contributions

Congress was generous in providing tax benefits for ESOPs, but there are limits. Generally, a C or an S corporation can deduct up to 25% of the total eligible payroll of plan participants to cover the principal portion of the loan, plus contributions to pay interest on the loan. In C corporations, the interest payments on the debt do not count toward the 25% of pay limit, provided the "one-third" test described below is met; in S corporations they do.

Eligible pay is currently defined as pay not exceeding $205,000 per year (as of 2004; this figure is indexed annually for inflation, rounding in $5,000 increments). Note that eligible pay only includes people actually in the plan. In many "Section 1042" transactions, sellers, 25% shareholders, and certain relatives of these individuals are not included in the plan, nor are most new employees and others not yet eligible to participate.

In addition, dividends paid on shares acquired by the ESOP loan in a C corporation can be used to repay the loan, and these are not included in the 25%-of-pay calculations. Dividends used to repay a loan must release additional shares (from the suspense account if there are enough; from other corporate shares if not) to employee accounts with a value equal to the dividends. If employees leave the company before they have a fully vested right to their shares, their forfeitures, which are allocated to everyone else, are not counted in the percentage limitations. Theoretically, total payments made to the ESOP to repay a loan do not have to be adjusted downward because of other benefit contributions, but limits on how much individuals can get usually make this irrelevant. Employee deferrals to a 401(k) plan now count as eligible pay.

After a 2004 IRS private letter ruling, it seems clear that in C corporations (but not in S corporations), the 25% limit for deductible contributions to repay principal is *in addition* to contributions to other defined contribution plans, rather than being combined with them.

In evaluating limitations on contributions, it is important to understand that in addition to the deductible contribution limits based on the total amount of pay of plan participants as described above, there are limits on the amounts that can be received by any individual.

First, no one ESOP participant can receive more than 100% of pay in any year from principal payments on the loan, or more than $41,000 (as of 2004; this figure is adjusted annually for inflation in $1,000 increments), whichever is less. This aspect of plan limitations is called the "annual addition" limit or the "Section 415 limit" (after the Internal Revenue Code section where it is found). In calculating pay, amounts over $205,000 (as of 2004) for any individual are excluded. Contributions that do not meet these limits are forfeited and reallocated to other plan participants. Second, the limits include company contributions to other defined contribution plans. Employee contributions to benefit plans are also counted toward this 100% of pay or $41,000 (as of 2004) figure.

Third, the interest is excludable from the annual addition limits for C corporations only if not more than one-third of the benefits are allocated to highly compensated employees, as defined by Code Section 414 (q). If the one-third rule is not met, forfeitures are also counted in determining how much an employee is getting each year. In S corporations, interest always counts. Once an ESOP loan is repaid, forfeitures must count toward the annual individual account additions limits.

The effect of these provisions is that companies must very carefully assess just how much they can afford to borrow through the ESOP. Plans that violate these rules can suffer severe penalties, including plan disqualification. If payroll is inadequate, however, companies do have alternatives. The initial loan can be for less than the amount optimally desired, with a successor loan paying the rest. It may be possible to negotiate a longer loan period in order to stretch out contributions. Finally, and most importantly, companies can use dividends to repay the loan.

Using Dividends to Repay the Loan

C corporations (but not S corporations) can take a tax deduction when using dividend payments to repay the ESOP loan. These payments are not included in any of the calculations described above. Dividends on both allocated and unallocated shares are normally used to repay the loan. The dividends must be "reasonable." While this term has never been defined, most consultants believe it is a percentage of share value consistent with what other companies in the industry would pay given similar levels of profits. The dividends also must not be so high as to provide employees with "unreasonably" high compensation. The payment of excessive dividends will cause the dividends to be taxed, although it is not certain whether only the excess dividends or the entire dividend will be taxed. In extreme cases, the plan can be disqualified. Nonetheless, some very profitable companies can use dividends to increase the percentage of pay going to an ESOP to 50% or more.

Many companies use preferred stock in their ESOPs to allow for higher dividend payments. Whatever kind of stock is used, the amount of the dividends must be allocated to employee accounts.

Companies normally allocate these amounts in the form of shares released from the suspense account. For dividends paid on allocated shares and used to repay the loan, the value of the shares released must be at least equal to the amount of dividends used. That means that allocations of these shares to employees will be equal to the ratio of their account balance to the prior total amount in the plan. Dividends on unallocated shares that are used to repay the loan can be allocated on this same basis, on the basis of relative compensation, or according to some more equal formula. The allocation must occur in the year the dividend is used to repay the loan.

Using Dividends in S Corporations to Repay the Loan

Most S corporations make distributions of part of their earnings, usually to help owners pay their taxes. In an ESOP S corporation, distributions received by the ESOP on both allocated and unallocated shares can be used to repay the ESOP loan (as well as for other purposes, including to repurchase shares or simply add diversity to employee accounts).

Other Issues

The rules for leveraged ESOPs are similar to the rules of other qualified plans in terms of participation, allocation, vesting, and distribution, but several special considerations apply.

How Shares Get to Employees

All employees over 21 who work for more than 1,000 hours in a plan year must be included in the plan unless they are covered by a collective bargaining unit, are in a separate line of business of at least 50 employees not covered by the ESOP, or fall into one of several anti-discrimination exemptions not commonly used by leveraged ESOPs. If there is a union, the company must bargain in good faith with it over inclusion in the plan if the union wants to discuss the issue. Companies may want to include union employees in leveraged plans to maximize the amount of eligible payroll. If the ESOP does not replace other benefits, this normally can be done without requiring a reopening of the contract.

As shares are released from the suspense account, they are allocated to individual employee accounts. This allocation can be on the basis of relative compensation (generally, all W-2 compensation is counted), but a more equal formula can also be used, such as per capita or seniority, or some combination. These other formulas must be written in such a way, however, that no highly compensated individual gets more than would be allocated under a relative pay formula. If a more level formula is used, remember that it restricts eligible pay. For example, if pay over $50,000 is not used, total pay over that amount is not included in calculating the total eligible payroll for the various contribution limits. In some cases, this may mean there is not sufficient eligible payroll to amortize the loan through the ESOP.

The allocated shares are subject to vesting. Employees must be 100% vested after five years of service (cliff vesting), or the company can use a graduated vesting schedule not slower than 20% after three years and 20% per year more until 100% is reached after seven years. If the ESOP is structured as part of a 401(k) plan, vesting must be complete within six years. If the ESOP contribution is used as a match to employee 401(k) deferrals (whether the ESOP and 401(k) are integrated or not), and the match is used to meet the "safe harbor" antidiscrimination rules for 401(k) plans, the contributions must vest immediately. Generally, if a company contributes 3% or more to the accounts of all eligible 401(k) participants (whether they make deferrals or not) or matches at a rate of at least 100% for the first 3% of pay employees defer, and 50% for the next 2%, then it does not have to test for participation in the 401(k) plan.

When employees reach age 55 and have 10 years of participation in the plan, the company must either give them the option of diversifying 25% of their account balances among at least three other investment alternatives or must simply pay the amount out to the employees. This option extends for each of the next four years. The diversification limit applies to the total share value in the participant's account (not the total account balance, part of which may already be diversified). If a participant chooses to diversify part or all of the eligible 25% in any year, an additional amount in each subsequent year can be diversified so that the total amount of shares diversified is 25%. Thus, an employee could diversify 25% of subsequent stock allocations, but could not diversify 25% of the total allocations in year one, then 25% of what is left in the account year two, etc. (this incorrect approach would result in over 75% diversification in year five). In the sixth year, eligible employees can increase their diversification to 50%.

When employees retire, die, or are disabled, the company must distribute their vested shares to them not later than the last day of the plan year following the year of their departure. For employees leaving before reaching retirement age, distribution must begin not later than the last day of the sixth plan year following their year of separation from service. Payments can be in substantially equal installments over five years or in a lump sum. In the installment method, a company normally pays out a portion of the stock from the trust each year. The value of the stock may go up or down over that time, of course. In a lump-sum distribution, the company buys the shares at their current value but can make the purchase in installments over five years as long as it provides adequate security and reasonable interest. If a distribution is over $830,000 (as of 2004), the five-year period can be extended by one year for each additional $165,000 (as of 2004), up to five additional years (these amounts are indexed yearly). Distributions are generally made in stock or cash, but the participant has the right to demand shares. ESOP shares must be valued at least annually by an independent outside appraiser unless the shares are publicly traded.

There are two important exceptions to these requirements. If a company's charter or bylaws state that all or substantially all of the company's stock must be held by employees (inside or outside the ESOP), or the company is an S corporation, the company can require the employees to take the cash value of the stock. Second, leveraged ESOPs can delay the start of repayment until the loan is repaid. There is an exception to this exception, though. Payment must begin not later than the 60th day following the plan year in which an employee who has separated from service reaches the plan's normal retirement age and has reached the 10th anniversary of starting to participate in the plan.

Finally, private companies and some thinly traded public companies must repurchase the shares from departing employees at their fair market value, as determined by the appraiser. This so-called "put option" can be exercised by the employee in one of two 60-day periods, one starting when the employee receives the distribution and the second period one year after that. The employee can choose which one to use. This obligation should be considered at the outset of the ESOP process and factored into the company's ability to repay the loan.

Within these limits, as long as a company does not discriminate between employees, it can set its own distribution requirements.

Voting Rules

Voting is one of the most controversial and least understood of ESOP issues. The trustee of the ESOP actually votes the ESOP shares. The question is "who directs the trustee?" The trustee can make the decision independently, although that is very rare. Alternatively, management or the ESOP administrative committee can direct the trustee, or the trustee can follow employee directions.

In private companies, employees must be able to direct the trustee as to the voting of shares *allocated* to their accounts on several key issues, including closing, sale, liquidation, recapitalization, and other issues having to do with the basic structure of the company. These general rules may differ in how they apply to specific cases, however. In public companies, employees must be able to vote on all issues. Private companies have the option of passing through voting rights on a one-person, one-vote basis.

Voting rights are more complicated than they seem, however. First, voting is not the same as tendering shares. So while employees may be required to vote on all issues, they may have no say about whether shares are tendered. In public companies, this is a major issue. Almost all public companies now write their plans to give employees the right to direct the tendering, as well as voting, of their shares, for reasons explained below.

Second, employees need not be given the right to direct the voting of unallocated shares. In a leveraged ESOP, this means that for the first several years of the loan, the trustee can vote the majority of the shares, if that is what the company wants to do. The company could provide that unallocated shares, as well as any allocated shares for which the trustee has not received instructions, should be voted or tendered in proportion to the allocated shares for which directions were received.

Third, if employees vote their shares on all issues, a company can still restrict their voting rights. The major issue on which employees would vote, of course, is who sits on the board of directors. A company could amend its bylaws to restrict who can be nominated for the board, thus retaining control within a management group, if desired.

The concern with voting rights may be more smoke than fire, however. Research by the NCEO indicates that employees are very conservative shareholders who normally support existing management. In a recent Gallup poll, 56% to 71% of people surveyed said if they were employee owners, they would prefer to let management make decisions on a variety of corporate issues. Managers of companies that are employee-owned and employee-controlled say that employee voting rights have made very little difference in how their companies actually run. Of course, there are always exceptions, and these can cause legitimate management concern.

Unlike private companies, public companies usually want employees to direct the voting and tendering of shares. That is because trustees in an ESOP may see their role as maximizing the share value of the plan's holdings, thus causing them to accept an offer by an unwanted suitor. Employees, however, will probably (but not always) vote against a raider. In a key court decision, a Delaware judge ruled that if employees can independently direct the voting and tendering of the shares, an ESOP may be an effective defense against a takeover. There are many other considerations here, however.

Military Leave

In the case of employees on military leave, employers must comply with the Uniformed Services Employment and Reemployment Rights Act (USERRA). By law, for all retirement plan benefits, employees must continue to receive vesting as if they still worked for the company. There is no break in service. Employers are not required to make contributions or allocate forfeitures during the time of service, however. If there is a 401(k) plan, the employee has the right, over the lesser of five years or three times the length of employment, to make make-up contributions, and the employer would have to match these according to the formula that otherwise would have applied.

Accounting and Reporting Issues

Accounting for ESOPs is covered elsewhere in this book, but the basics can be outlined here.

The debt acquired by the ESOP must be counted as corporate debt, even if the corporation is able to get the loan without guaranteeing it. Until the late 1980s, banks often could obtain unguaranteed loans for their ESOPs and use the ESOP purchase of their shares to increase their capital, but this is no longer an acceptable accounting practice.

The offsetting debit to the liability recorded by the employer should show up as a reduction in shareholder equity (it appears as a contra equity account). The argument here is that the shares in the ESOP are held by a third party but are not yet paid for. As the loan is repaid and shares are released, both the liability and the offsetting contra equity account are reduced.

Amounts contributed or committed to be contributed to the ESOP need to be reported, with contributions to cover principal charged to compensation expense and interest accounted for as it normally would be allocated. Shares held by the ESOP are deemed as outstanding for calculations of earnings per share. For plans started after January 1, 1993, the value of shares released is their current market value. Plans started before then can use the acquisition cost or market value. Dividends should be charged to retained earnings except when dividends are used to repay a loan. Then they are charged to retained earnings for allocated shares and current earnings for unallocated shares. Where the principal-only method of repaying the loan is used, it may be necessary to take a charge to earnings equivalent to what the principal and interest method would produce.

These guidelines are based on the position of the American Institute of Certified Public Accountants (AICPA). Most were adopted by the Financial Accounting Standards Board in 1989. They are not laws or regulations, but standard accepted practices. Some accountants differ on one or more of these points.

On a related issue, the Securities and Exchange Commission ruled in December 1989 that the MacMillan Company should have reported that the ESOP it planned to create in 1987 was meant as an anti-takeover device. The SEC opined that any time an ESOP buys more than 5% of the shares in a public company and the ESOP has anti-takeover purposes, this must be reported. Of course, companies almost always deny this is what they have in mind, so this has been an issue of considerable contention.

Issues for S Corporations

Since January 1, 1998, S corporations have been able to have an ESOP own stock in the company. Tax law changes in 1996 and 1997 made this possible, first by allowing ESOPs and certain other non-taxable trusts to own shares in S corporations, provided they pay tax on profits attributable to them as unrelated business income. The 1996 law, however, allowed employees to receive a distribution of their shares when they leave the company. That could lead to a disqualification of the company's S status if the employees rolled the stock into an IRA or if the number of shareholders exceeded 75 (the maximum number of shareholders for an S corporation at that time; for tax years beginning after 2004, the limit is now 100).

In 1997, Congress changed the law to allow S corporations to require that employees take the cash equivalent value of their shares when they receive their distributions. Certain other technical problems were fixed as well. More important, the new law specifically and exclusively exempted ESOPs from the unrelated business income tax (UBIT). In other words, whatever percentage of the company the ESOP owns would not be subject to any current taxation.

On the other hand, the new law did not provide S corporation ESOPs with the same tax benefits available to C corporation ESOPs. Specifically, (1) owners of S corporation stock cannot use the tax-deferred Section 1042 rollover when selling to an ESOP, (2) dividends (i.e., S corporation "distributions") used to repay a loan or passed through to participants are not deductible, and (3) interest payments on an ESOP loan count toward the contribution limits. Moreover, contribution limits were set at 15% of pay for plan years not starting after December 31, 2001, not the 25% available to leveraged ESOPs for principal payments on an ESOP loan. As noted above, this figure went up to 25% for plan years after that.

In 2001, Congress added a complex new provision for S corporations to prevent abuses of the non-taxability of the ESOP's ownership interest. The good news for the large majority of S corporation ESOPs is that this will not affect them in any way. It will, however, prevent ESOPs from being used in S corporations to benefit just a few usually highly paid people. Specifically, the law defines certain ESOP participants as "disqualified persons." These are individuals who own more than 10% of the shares in the ESOP, counting allocated shares, their pro-rata share of unallocated shares, and, outside the ESOP, any stock options or other synthetic equity (this includes, among other things, a variety of kinds of deferred compensation). Direct ownership does not count. They also include people who, using family attribution rules, own more than 20% of the shares this way. If these individuals collectively own more than

50% of the company, including their ownership of synthetic equity, direct ownership, and their ESOP ownership, then they cannot receive allocations form the ESOP. If they do, there is a 50% excise tax on the allocations and on any synthetic equity, and the allocations are counted as taxable income to them.

Valuation Issues

A separate chapter in this book deals with valuation concerns, but a few should be noted here. The fact of leveraging the ESOP may decrease the value of the shares because of the new debt, but not necessarily on a dollar-for-dollar basis. Valuation involves more issues than just the book value of the company, and these may provide additional value even after a 100% buyout. Although the company would have no net asset value after such a transaction, it still would have the capacity to earn income, and this provides some level of value. Second, the valuation should reflect the ongoing repurchase obligation. If it does not, then the shares will be overpriced; the obligation is a legal one and a very real liability to the company.

Freezing or Terminating an ESOP

Each year, 3% to 4% of all ESOPs are terminated; an unknown percentage are frozen, usually because the sponsor wants to create a different kind of benefit plan, wants to recapture some of the ESOP's ownership, or, more rarely, has financial problems. Terminating or freezing a plan is a decision that can be made by the plan sponsor, but, in both cases, there are special considerations that need to be taken into account.

Freezing an ESOP

In a frozen plan, further contributions to the plan stop, but the plan continues to operate. Employees receive their distributions according to the rules of the plan document. Theoretically, the plan could continue until the last participant receives a distribution. As in all ESOP matters, the ESOP committee or other fiduciary should be careful to document and justify all decisions.

At first blush, it may seem that freezing the plan is the simplest step when a company wants to wind down its ESOP. There are, however, a number of problems freezing can create. First, the plan must still be administered, with annual reports to participants and the government. In closely held companies, there must be an annual valuation. Top-heavy rules (i.e., rules imposed on plans in which highly compensated employees' accounts exceed 60% of the total employee accounts) must still be met. Remaining participants still get to partake in any stock appreciation. Any improprieties in the plan could lead to lawsuits. These additional costs and risks may more than offset the benefits from not simply terminating the plan and paying people out, as discussed below.

Terminating an ESOP

When a plan is terminated, all participants become fully vested, and distributions must begin within a year of the plan's termination. Payouts for the distributions can be made in equal installments with adequate security over five years (or more in cases of distributions over $830,000, as of 2004; this figure is indexed each year). Alternatively, the amounts can be rolled over into a successor plan, such as a 401(k) or profit sharing plan. The company could make the rollover mandatory, or it could give employees an option. Participants must have the right to receive their distribution in stock if they so choose unless the plan calls for cash distributions and all or substantially all the company's stock is owned by employees.

In a nonleveraged plan or a leveraged plan where the loan is fully repaid, the amounts that are allocated are paid out directly to participants or rolled over into a successor plan. Terminating a leveraged plan where the loan has not yet been repaid is more complicated. To repay the loan, the company must reacquire the shares or sell them to another buyer. If the shares are not at a price that repays the remaining amount, the company makes up the difference; if selling the shares results in more cash than is needed, a more complicated situation arises. An amount equal to the basis paid for the shares divided by the proceeds of the sale, multiplied by the excess after the loan is paid off, must be allocated to employee accounts on the basis of their relative share balances. In other words, any windfall from the shares goes to employee accounts.

Terminating or freezing a plan is not a decision to be taken lightly. There are important fiduciary issues to consider that should be discussed carefully with qualified counsel.

Should You Undertake a Leveraged ESOP?

Obviously, leveraged ESOPs are complicated and carry many obligations and restrictions. Their benefits are also substantial, however. So how does a company decide whether an ESOP is worthwhile, or, given that, whether a leveraged or nonleveraged ESOP would be more advantageous?

Before deciding on a leveraged ESOP, it is worth considering a nonleveraged ESOP. Some companies may not have the ability to obtain or repay a loan, or they may simply be averse to debt. In other cases, the company may not want to be constrained by a debt repayment schedule, instead preferring to make periodic discretionary cash or stock contributions to the ESOP. This means shares will be bought out more slowly, but if they being bought from existing owners, this may be acceptable if the owners are not in any rush to sell or think the stock price will rise over time.

A primary reason for using leverage is to enable the ESOP to acquire enough stock (30% of the company) to qualify sellers for the tax deferral of Section 1042. Some companies do this by accumulating cash contributions in the ESOP until there is enough to meet this goal (as noted above, this generally can be done for a few years), or putting in some cash, then borrowing the rest.

If an ESOP is used to borrow money, several issues need to be considered. First, companies need to consider any dilution effects the ESOP may create if the company is issuing new stock to the plan, rather than buying back existing shares. Most ESOPs do not issue new shares, however.

Second, companies need to evaluate carefully what the tax benefits of the plan will be (remember that all these benefits have no value to unprofitable corporations) and whether they will have adequate cash flow to service the debt. This may seem obvious, but in several cases, leveraged ESOPs have been used to buy out an owner, leaving the employees with more debt than they could handle, and their companies have closed.

Third, alternative forms of financing should be considered. The long-term benefits of an ESOP are hotly debated by experts solely concerned with their corporate financial impact. Equity or even straight debt may be preferable in some cases. That is especially the case when companies seriously consider (as too many do not) the repurchase obligation. ESOPs have up-front cash flow benefits, but require a long-term liability.

Fourth, public companies must consider the impact of the ESOP on shareholder relations. Leveraged ESOPs can make their financial reports look worse, unless offset by changes in other benefit plans. Yet these changes may have an undesired impact on employee morale.

Fifth, the size of the payroll relative to the size of the ESOP must be considered. ESOPs may simply not work in some companies because their total compensation is too small. While some companies may expect growth to solve the problem, lenders may take a more skeptical look at just how likely growth really is. For some companies, the answer to this may be a nonleveraged ESOP. This allows much greater flexibility in determining when and if to make contributions. The company can contribute as little or as much as it wants within applicable limits, however. This means, of course, that shares will be acquired more gradually, rather than bought all at once with a loan repaid over several years.

Finally, in any ESOP, but especially in one where the financial commitment is as fixed as a leveraged plan, ESOPs should never be installed solely because their tax benefits look appealing. Unless managers and owners are comfortable with and committed to the concept of employee ownership, an ESOP is not a good choice. Other financing and benefit plans offer tax breaks of their own. What ESOPs do is allow companies to share ownership with employees at the same time that they are financing other corporate objectives. But if a company is concerned only with the latter issue, and regrets the requirement of the former, eventually the ESOP will be seen as a mistake. ESOPs work best when companies share information, communicate about the plan regularly, and get employee owners more involved in the day-to-day decisions affecting their work. Absent these efforts, an ESOP is just another benefit plan and may not be the best one for any of the parties involved.

Chapter 2

Contribution and Allocation Limits for Leveraged ESOPs

Luis Granados

Over the past 30 years, the United States Congress has gone to great lengths to encourage the proliferation of employee stock ownership plans (ESOPs). Over a dozen separate federal laws have been enacted to encourage corporations to provide stock ownership to their employees through ESOPs.

The Tax Reform Act of 1984 ("TRA '84") stands as the watershed legislation in terms of tax incentives intended to promote the growth of ESOPs. Included in TRA '84 were the following:

- Section 1042 of the Internal Revenue Code of 1954 (now the Internal Revenue Code of 1986 [the "Code"]), which allows certain shareholders of closely held corporations to sell stock to an ESOP and, provided they invest the sale proceeds in certain securities (stock or bonds) issued by other corporations and satisfy certain other requirements, defer (perhaps forever) federal taxation on any capital gain resulting from the sale; and

- Section 404(k) of the Code, which allows the sponsoring corporation to deduct, for federal income tax purposes, certain cash dividends that it pays on its stock held by an ESOP.

The Small Business Job Protection Act of 1996 and the Taxpayer Relief Act of 1997 for the first time allowed S corporation stock to be held by an ESOP and created substantial tax advantages for S corporations with large ESOP ownership positions. Most recently, the Economic Growth and Tax Relief Reconciliation Act of 2001 substantially liberalized the rules governing ESOPs and other employee benefit plans.

At least partly as a result of this and other federal legislation, the number of ESOPs in the United States has increased from 300 in 1974, the year of enactment of the Employee Retirement Income Security Act of 1974 (ERISA)[1] to over 11,000 as of 2004.[2] When one recognizes that almost nine million working men and women now own stock in their employer corporations through ESOPs, one must conclude that Congress has begun to accomplish its objective.

As the ESOP concept has matured, especially since TRA '84, ESOPs have acquired increasingly larger portions of large and small companies. In so doing, they have had to address the various rules imposed upon ESOPs and other qualified plans by ERISA and the Code, including the limits imposed by Sections 404 and 415 of the Code.

ESOPs Described

An ESOP may consist of a stock bonus plan or a combination of a stock bonus plan and a money purchase pension plan.[3] It is intended to comply with the provisions of the Code and ERISA that apply to other defined contribution plans. For example, it is generally subject to the same eligibility, participation, nondiscrimination, and vesting provisions of the Code, and the same general fiduciary responsibility provisions of ERISA, as are other defined contribution plans.

The major points at which an ESOP departs from other defined contribution plans are that it must be designed to invest primarily in employer securities,[4] and that it may incur indebtedness, involving a guarantee or other extension of credit by a "party in interest" under Section 3(14) of ERISA or a "disqualified person" under Section 4975(e)(2) of the Code, for the purchase of such employer securities. It is this ability of the ESOP to borrow funds to purchase employer securities that gives it the unique position of being both a qualified retirement plan and, as recognized by the IRS, a "technique of corporate finance."[5]

An ESOP can acquire stock of the employer corporation in three different ways. First, the corporation can issue and contribute shares of newly issued or treasury stock to the ESOP each year. These contributions of stock are tax-deductible to the corporation within the limits set forth in Section 404(a) of the Code, as described below. Second, the ESOP can accumulate cash contributed by the corporation and purchase stock from the corporation or its shareholders. Third, the ESOP may use borrowed funds to purchase shares of employer stock from the corporation and/or from one or more selling shareholders. The borrowing of funds can be effected by the issuance by the ESOP of a promissory note to the corporation or selling shareholder(s) in exchange for the acquired stock; alternatively, funds for the purchase can be loaned by a third party directly to the ESOP, supported by a guarantee of the ESOP's indebtedness by the corporation or the selling shareholder(s). Another common structure is for there to be a loan from a third-party lender to the corporation, which in turn loans the money to the ESOP to purchase stock.

If the ESOP is leveraged, i.e., if it borrows money to purchase stock, each year during the ESOP's amortization of its acquisition indebtedness, the corporation usually contributes (and/or pays cash dividends) to the ESOP in sufficient amounts to allow the ESOP to make timely payments thereon. These amounts are also tax-deductible to the employer corporation within the limits set forth in Section 404 of the Code, as described below.

For these reasons, chief among the provisions of the Code that are applicable to ESOPs and other qualified plans are the limits under Section 404 of the Code on the amount that may be contributed to the ESOP and other such plans each year on a tax-deductible basis and the limits under Code Section 415 on the amount of contributions and forfeitures that may be added to the account of any individual participating employee in a year under the ESOP and all other such plans maintained by the employer. These are two of the key provisions of the Code that can limit the ability of employees to use a leveraged ESOP to purchase stock in their companies. These limitations were substantially liberalized in the Economic Growth and Tax Relief Reconciliation Act of 2001 (EGTRRA), which is generally effective for plan years beginning after 2002. The purpose of this chapter is to discuss these limits, both before and after giving effect to the 2001 tax law, and their effect on ESOPs, especially leveraged ESOPs.

Code Section 404

As stated above, Section 404 of the Code limits the amount that can be contributed to an ESOP and all other qualified plans maintained by an employer corporation in any year. All such contributions by the employer are included in this limit. Before 2002,[6] all tax-deferred contributions by employees to a "cash or deferred arrangement" under Section 401(k) of the Code were also included in this limit, but these amounts are now excluded (although employer matching and discretionary contributions are still counted).

Under Section 404(a)(3) of the Code, tax-deductible contributions to all stock bonus plans and profit sharing plans of an employer corporation generally cannot exceed 15% of the compensation of all participating employees before 2002; after 2001, however, this figure is increased to 25%. For purposes of Section 404 of the Code, an employee's compensation that may be taken into account may not exceed $150,000 per year, as adjusted for increases in the cost of living. For 2002, the limit was increased to $200,000, and it is indexed for inflation;[7] for 2004, the limit is $205,000.[8]

Section 404(a)(7) increased the deduction limit for plan years before 2002 to 25% of the compensation of all participating employees if the employer contributed to a pension plan in addition to the stock bonus or profit sharing plan (such as an ESOP that consists of a stock bonus plan and a money purchase pension plan, which is considered a pension plan for this purpose). Now, however (i.e., for plan years beginning in 2002), the limit for defined contribution plans standing alone is 25% of compensation, so the Section 404(a)(7) rule is meaningless in most cases.

Companies that previously added a money purchase pension portion to their ESOPs in order to take advantage of this rule may merge the money purchase pension portion into the stock bonus portion of the ESOP (effectively eliminating the money purchase portion) without triggering 100% vesting on "termination" of the money purchase pension plan. [9] Companies with pre-EGTRRA ESOPs that include a money purchase pension plan feature can terminate this feature by following the procedures outlined in Rev. Rul. 2002-42, including, but not limited to, providing a special notice to each participant describing the elimination of the feature.[10]

In addition, Section 404(a)(3)(A)(v) of the Code provides that if an employer maintained one or more qualified plans before plan years beginning on or after January 1, 1987, and contributed less than the maximum tax-deductible amount to those plans in one or more years, the unused contribution amount may be carried forward and added to the contributions under Code Section 404(a)(3) to increase the tax-deductible contributions to 25% of the compensation of all participating employees. After 2001, the value of this rule has been curtailed, as the defined contribution plan deduction limitation will be increased to 25% of compensation in any event.

Applying these limits to an ESOP, their effect is easily seen. Before 2002, if the compensation of employees participating in a stock bonus plan and/or profit sharing plan was $1,000,000 per year, the employer's tax-deductible contributions were limited to $150,000 per year; if an ESOP consisted of a stock bonus plan and a money purchase plan, the employer's tax-deductible contribution could be as high as $250,000 per year. As of 2002, the deductible contributions have been $250,000 per year regardless of whether a money purchase plan is used.

Before 2002, if the employer also maintained a defined contribution plan including a "cash or deferred arrangement" under Section 401(k) of the Code, or if the ESOP included such an arrangement, amounts that the employees deferred into the 401(k) portion counted toward these limits. Even worse, the amounts that employees deferred into the 401(k) portion reduced their compensation taken into account to determine the maximum contribution under Section 404 of the Code. For example, if employees in the above example contributed $100,000 to a 401(k) plan, tax-deductible contributions would be limited to 15% (or 25%) of $900,000, not $1 million. The ESOP contribution would then be aggregated with the $100,000 to determine whether the limits were exceeded. Both of these rules were changed starting in 2002: employee salary deferrals do not count against the deductible contribution limit, and they are added back to the compensation base in computing the denominator of that limit. In the above example, the employees could defer as much of their salaries as they want to the 401(k) plan, and the employer will still be able to deduct $250,000 for its contribution to the ESOP.

As a general rule, if an ESOP borrows money to purchase employer stock, a third-party lender may be reluctant to have that indebtedness outstanding for more than seven years. Therefore, if the intention is to leverage the ESOP to purchase stock and enable the ESOP to repay its indebtedness using 100% tax-deductible contributions from the corporation, absent some other rules that are applicable to the ESOP, it would be necessary to be sure that the amount that the ESOP has borrowed can be repaid within these tax-deductible limits over a seven-year period.

To encourage employers to leverage ESOPs in larger amounts, Code Section 404(a)(9) was enacted in 1981. This provides that, notwithstanding the employer corporation's contributions under Code Sections 404(a)(3) and 404(a)(7), a C corporation may contribute up to 25% of the compensation of participating employees to enable a leveraged ESOP to pay principal on its indebtedness and to contribute, again on a tax-deductible basis, any additional amounts necessary for the ESOP to pay all interest on its indebtedness. Put another way, absent any other limiting factor under the Code, the existence of another qualified plan, such as a defined benefit pension plan or a profit sharing plan, would not inhibit the employer corporation's ability to service the ESOP's acquisition indebtedness with contributions on a 100% tax-deductible basis, up to 25% of compensation, with no limit on contributions used to pay interest on the acquisition debt.

The usefulness of Section 404(a)(9) for C corporations is not eliminated by the 2001 tax law. Although it will no longer be necessary to rely on Section 404(a)(9) to increase deductions up to 25% of compensation, the ability to deduct unlimited amounts contributed to the ESOP and used to pay interest on a stock acquisition loan remains of great value, particularly in the early years of a loan when the interest payments are quite high. Moreover, the wording of Section 404(a)(9) appears to permit total deductions to qualified plans far in excess of 25% of compensation, since it permits a 25% of compensation deduction for contributions used to pay principal on an ESOP loan *in addition to* the 25% of compensation deduction available for other defined contribution plans. The IRS applied this reasoning in PLR 9548036 (September 7, 1995), and IRS representatives have indicated in public forums that Section 404(a)(9) provides a separate authority for deductions from the authority provided under Section 404(a)(3). PLR 200436015 (June 9, 2004) also concludes that a C corporation employer may contribute up to 12% of compensation to a money purchase pension plan and up to 3.5% of compensation in matching contributions to a 401(k) plan at the same time that it is contributing up to 25% of compensation to its leveraged ESOP to make principal payments on a loan.[11]

Neither of these rulings addresses the case in which an employer attempts to deduct more than 25% of compensation to make principal payments on a loan, deducting 25% under Section 404(a)(9) and the balance under Section 404(a)(3). IRS representatives have informally indicated that this is not permitted. However, nothing in Section 404(a)(3) prevents contributions made under that section from being used to make payments on an ESOP loan, and S corporations (which cannot use Section 404(a)(9)) do so routinely. This issue may ultimately be resolved in court.

The ESOP must be established by the end of the relevant taxable year of the employer if it is to claim deductions for that year. Although Code Section 404(a)(9) does not expressly require the ESOP loan to be in place by that time for the employer to be able to deduct contributions, the IRS informally has taken the position that the indebtedness must have been incurred prior to the end of the taxable year in order to receive a deduction under Code Section 404(a)(9) for contributions made prior to the tax filing date that are applied to repay interest or principal on the loan.[12]

There are two penalties for exceeding the deduction limitations of Section 404: (1) the excess amounts are not deductible for the year in which they were made (although they may be carried forward and be deductible in a subsequent year), and (2) a 10% excise tax on the non-deductible amounts is applied under Code Section 4972. Although some S corporations that are 100% owned by an ESOP may not be concerned about the loss or deferral of deductions to a subsequent year, they should be concerned about the Section 4972 excise tax, which applies at the corporate level rather than at the shareholder level.

It is important to remember, though, that the deduction limits of Section 404 are only a part of the problem. Section 415 provides additional limits, with penalties even more severe than those that apply under Section 404.

Code Section 415

Section 415 of the Code limits the amount of total assets that may accrue to the benefit of a participant in a year in all qualified plans in which he or she participates. Failure to stay within the limits of Section 415 of the Code, by as little as one dollar, could disqualify the ESOP and cause horrendous consequences.[13]

Before 2002, Section 415(c) of the Code limited the amount of contributions and forfeitures that can be allocated to an employee's accounts under all defined contribution plans in which he or she participates to the lesser of 25% of his or her compensation or $30,000 (as adjusted in accordance with increases in the cost of living). These amounts, referred to as "annual additions," included all employer contributions, all employee tax-deferred and after-tax contributions, and all forfeitures added to a participant's account. Compensation is defined for this purpose by adding back employee salary deferrals to a 401(k) or cafeteria plan. After 2001, the limits increase to $40,000 (adjusted annually for inflation) or 100% of compensation. For plan years beginning after 2003, the inflation-adjusted dollar limit is increased to $41,000.

The inclusion of forfeitures within these limits was especially problematic for ESOPs in that forfeitures are not available to service the ESOP's acquisition indebtedness, and therefore limit the amount of money that the ESOP could borrow and repay using tax-deductible corporate dollars. Moreover, because the level of forfeitures is not predictable in advance, employers could not tell how large of a loan service their ESOPs could support. And because Section 404(j) of the Code provides that an employer may not deduct amounts it contributes to a defined contribution plan that cannot be allocated to participating employees' accounts due to the limits of Section 415 of the Code, the potential effect of the Section 415 limits on the employer's ability to make tax-deductible contributions to a leveraged ESOP, absent some exception to this provision, is clear.

To address this problem, Congress enacted Section 415(c)(6) of the Code. This provision provides that, so long as not more than one-third of the employer corporation's contributions to the ESOP (that are deductible under Section 404(a)(9) of the Code) to pay principal and interest on the ESOP's acquisition indebtedness in a year are allocated to the accounts of "highly compensated employees," as defined in Section 414(q) of the Code, the allocations to participants' accounts resulting from contributions to pay interest on the ESOP's indebtedness (that are deductible under Code Section 404(a)(9)) and forfeitures of ESOP shares acquired with the proceeds of a loan described in Section 404(a)(9)(A) are not deemed to be annual additions. In effect, at the same time that it created Section 404(a)(9) of the Code, Congress created Section 415(c)(6) of the Code to allow the maximum leveraging by employees for the acquisition of stock. Note that there is a question as to whether any part of the benefits of Section 415(c)(6) are available for S corporations, as discussed further below.

Ironically, under the law as in effect before 2002, the Section 415 limitations tended to be more important in practice than the Section

404 limitations. It was almost (but not quite) impossible to exceed the Section 404 limitations without first having violated Section 415, thereby disqualifying the entire plan. That situation is now reversed: it is easier to violate the 25% of compensation limit of Section 404 than it is to violate the 100% of compensation limit of Section 415. However, it is still possible to violate the $40,000 limit of Section 415 for individual highly paid employees.

Code Section 404(k)

To help alleviate the limiting effect of Sections 404 and 415 of the Code on leveraged ESOPs, in 1984 the Congress enacted Section 404(k) of the Code. As now in effect, this allows a C corporation to deduct, for federal income tax purposes, cash dividends it pays on shares of stock in an ESOP, to the extent the cash dividends are either (1) made available as taxable income to participants or, more importantly for purposes of this chapter, (2) applied by the ESOP to repay indebtedness it incurred to purchase the shares of stock on which the dividends are paid. Starting in 2002, dividends are also deductible if employees are given a choice whether to have them paid out in cash or have them reinvested in company stock.

For these dividends to be deductible, however, Section 404(k)(5) of the Code requires that they not be used as a method of tax "avoidance or evasion." From 1988 through 2001, the term used in this section was only "evasion," leaving out "avoidance." The legislative history of the 2001 tax law (as well as some pre-1988 legislative history) indicates that for a dividend not to constitute "avoidance or evasion," it must be "reasonable." Solely for purposes of determining the reasonableness of dividends deducted because participants were given the option of receiving them or having them reinvested in company stock, a "reasonable" dividend is deemed to be a dividend equal to that paid on common stock by the company, for a public company, or by similar publicly traded companies, for a closely held company. This means dividends on convertible preferred stock, which are typically higher than dividends on common stock, may not be deducted under this authority (although they may still be deductible if passed through in cash to the participants or used to make payments on an ESOP stock acquisition loan).

The corporate federal income tax deduction for cash dividends paid on stock in an ESOP is in addition to the deduction for contributions under Sections 404(a)(3), 404(a)(7), and 404(a)(9) of the Code. Further, because dividends represent earnings on the stock held by the ESOP rather than contributions or forfeitures, they are not included as "annual additions" under Section 415 of the Code. Therefore, the use of cash dividends clearly enhances the ability of the employer corporation to amortize a C corporation leveraged ESOP's acquisition indebtedness on a 100% tax-deductible basis.

There are two major limiting factors on the use of cash dividends for this purpose. First, only cash dividends that are paid on unallocated shares or allocated shares acquired *with the proceeds of a specific loan* may be used to repay that loan; dividends on shares acquired in a non-leveraged purchase and dividends on shares for which the acquisition indebtedness has already been repaid in full may *not* be used by the ESOP to repay an acquisition loan that is used to purchase new shares. This limitation became effective in August 1989. Dividends on shares acquired by an ESOP before that time may continue to be used to repay subsequent indebtedness, subject to general fiduciary considerations. The law becomes somewhat unclear where there are multiple lender financing transactions. For example, if ESOP shares are acquired partly with the proceeds of a bank loan and partly with a seller financing note that extends for a period beyond repayment of the bank loan, may dividends on the portion of the shares acquired with the bank loan be used to make payments on the seller note after the bank loan has been completely repaid? The rules are not clear.

Second, while such cash dividends are deductible to the corporation for federal income tax purposes, they are subject to alternative minimum tax. In effect, to the extent that the employer corporation's federal income tax is reduced due to the payment of tax-deductible dividends under Section 404(k) of the Code, it may nevertheless pay some minimum level of taxes, based on the amount of Code Section 404(k) dividends and other tax preference items that it enjoys.

Special Rules for S Corporations

The foregoing discussion applies primarily to regularly taxed C corporations. Since January 1, 1998, S corporations as defined in Section 1361 of the Code have, for the first time, been permitted to have ESOPs as owners of their stock. However, because of legislative

Section 404

Section 404(a)(9), which provides increased deduction limitations for contributions used to make payments on an ESOP loan, does not apply to S corporations. Therefore, the deduction limitation for contributions to S corporation ESOPs is limited to 25% of covered compensation, and contributions used to pay interest on the ESOP's debt are counted against this limit. Moreover, the apparent ability of a C corporation to take a deduction of up to 25% of compensation for making contributions to an ESOP that are used make principal payments on a loan, while at the same time contributing up to an additional 25% of compensation to another defined contribution plan, is not available for an S corporation.

Section 415

Section 415(c)(6), which provides increased annual addition limitations for leveraged ESOPs, is not expressly limited to C corporation ESOPs. However, it applies only to interest paid on a loan that is deductible under Section 404(a)(9)(B), which clearly cannot be used with an S corporation ESOP. It also applies to forfeitures of shares acquired with the proceeds of a loan "described in" Section 404(a)(9)(A). This creates some confusion, because all ESOP stock acquisition loans are "described in" Section 404(a)(9)(A). They are just not eligible for a deduction under that section, because of the limitations of Section 404(a)(9)(C). The IRS may take the position that forfeitures of S corporation leveraged shares do constitute annual additions, but employers have a fairly strong argument that they do not.

Section 404(k)

The dividend deduction under Section 404(k) is not available for S corporations. Before 2004, however, a serious issue for S corporations had been whether it was even permissible for the ESOP to use dividends[14] paid on shares that had been allocated to participant accounts to make payments on an ESOP loan. Dividends paid on unallocated shares in the loan suspense account could be used, but the IRS took the position that dividends paid on allocated shares in an S corporation ESOP could not be used to make ESOP stock acquisition loan payments.[15] In 2004, Congress effectively reversed this position by adding new Code Section 4975(f)(7),[16] explicitly stating that an S corporation ESOP may use S corporation distributions to make payments on a stock acquisition loan without violating the prohibited transaction or other rules governing an ESOP, in the same manner as C corporations. Moreover, Congress made this change retroactive to distributions paid after December 31, 1997, so that those who had unwittingly (or defiantly) acted contrary to the IRS position are protected by the new law.

Examples

Each of the following examples is based on the law applicable to plan years commencing after 2003.

Example I

ABC Engineering, Inc. ("ABC") is a C corporation with 150 employees and $14,750,000 in annual W-2 payroll, excluding amounts over $205,000 per employee. One hundred of its employees are rank-and-file workers who receive an average annual salary of $45,000. The remaining 50 employees are professionals who receive annual salaries of more than $205,000. ABC's outstanding common stock is valued at $15,000,000.

ABC Corp. decides to adopt an ESOP in which all of its employees participate. The ESOP enters into a direct loan agreement (the "Loan") with a bank to borrow $15,000,000. The Loan proceeds will be used to purchase 100% of the stock of ABC's sole shareholder. The bank requires the Loan to be repaid in five years. Assuming an 8% interest rate and a mortgage-type level payment amortization schedule, equal annual payments of principal and interest of $3,756,847 will be required for each of the five years. The maximum payment of principal will be in the fifth year, when $3,478,562 of the payment will constitute principal.

Because ABC's ESOP is leveraged, Section 404(a)(9) of the Code permits ABC to make annual principal repayment contributions of up to 25% of ABC's $14,750,000 participant compensation base (i.e., contributions totaling $3,687,500). Because the required principal payments for each Loan year are less than this amount, and because ABC can contribute as much as it wants on a tax-deductible basis to pay Loan interest, ABC will have no trouble servicing the Loan from a Code Section 404 deductibility viewpoint.

ABC will also be able to satisfy Section 415(c)'s annual addition limitations, because it can allocate to each participant's account the lesser of 100% of compensation or $41,000. The 50 highly paid employees can receive the maximum allocation of $41,000 each, for a total of $2,050,000, or 20% of their eligible compensation. If the remaining 100 nonhighly compensated employees receive an allocation of $1,706,847, or approximately 38% of their total $4,500,000 compensation, there will be enough money allocable each year to service the $3,756,847 annual payment requirement without violating Section 415. This example would not qualify for the special rule of Section 415(c)(6) allowing the plan to ignore interest payments in computing annual additions because it would not satisfy the one-third test for highly-compensated employees, but it does not need the benefit of that rule to avoid violating Section 415. (Note that the one-third test does not apply to the deduction rules under Section 404.) If a substantial amount of forfeitures have to be reallocated during the loan repayment period, however, there might be a problem, since the allocation of forfeitures will not be shielded by Section 415(c)(6).

Example 2

If the value of ABC corporation were higher, then it might be possible to comply with the Section 415 annual limits, but not with the Section 404 deduction limits. For example, if value were $20 million, then starting in the second year of loan payments the principal portion of the payment ($3,651,859, rising to $4,638,082 in the final year) would exceed the 25% of eligible compensation ($3,687,500) limitation. In such a case, ABC may want to consider paying dividends to the ESOP to enable it to service its debt in order to avoid imposition of the 10% excise tax under Section 4972 on nondeductible contributions. Dividends are earnings on plan assets, not employer contributions, and therefore are not subject to the Section 404 deduction limits or considered as annual additions for Section 415 purposes. If ABC pays the ESOP a modest 5.5% dividend, that would provide an extra $1.1 million that could be used for debt service that does not count against the Section 404 or Section 415 limitations.

Example 3

Assume again the facts of Example 2, but that ABC elects to become an S corporation. The use of dividends to repay the Loan would become less attractive, even though it is still permitted, because unlike contributions the dividends are not deductible for an S corporation. There may still be a way to avoid Section 4972 excise taxes without relying on dividends, by using a "back to back" loan structure (which most banks prefer anyway, so that they do not have to worry about compliance with the ESOP exempt loan regulations). Instead of loaning $20 million to the ESOP for a five-year term, the bank would loan the same amount to ABC Corp. for the same five-year term. ABC Corp. would then turn around and reloan the $20 million of bank loan proceeds to the ESOP, but on a somewhat longer loan repayment schedule. For example, if the loan from ABC to the ESOP had a seven-year term, then the total annual payment would be $3,841,448, and the maximum principal portion of that payment would be $3,556,896, which is less than the applicable Section 404 deduction limit.

Conclusion

The special ESOP rules in Sections 404(a)(9), 404(k), and 415(c)(6) facilitate payments to ESOPs that can be used to retire stock acquisition indebtedness—payments that are substantially larger than are permitted for other types of qualified plans, even in the post-2001 environment. With careful planning, it is possible for a C corporation ESOP to use these rules to acquire very large percentages of the stock of the sponsoring employer. Since some of these new rules do not apply to S corporation ESOPs, however, loans to S corporation ESOPs will either have to be reduced in size or lengthened in term in order to comply.

Notes

1. P.L. 93-406.
2. Source: The National Center for Employee Ownership.
3. Code § 4975(e)(7)(A).
4. The term "qualifying employer securities" is defined at Code § 4975(e)(8) to mean "employer securities" within the meaning of Code § 409(l).
5. Rev. Rul. 79-122, 1979-1 CB 204.
6. The 2001 tax act is actually effective for *plan years* beginning after December 31, 2001. Thus, all references in this chapter to the effects of the new law assume that the plan involved is on the calendar year. For a plan on a fiscal year, the changes will be effective for the plan year commencing during 2002.
7. Code § 401(a)(17).
8. Internal Revenue News Release IR-2003-122 , October 16, 2003.
9. Rev. Rul. 2002-42, I.R.B. 2002-28, July 15, 2002, p. 76.
10. Code § 4980F.
11. The contribution percentages for the three plans are deleted in the publicly available copies of this ruling but have been made available to the author.
12. Code § 404(a)(6) permits an employer to treat a contribution made before the due date for filing its tax return (including extensions) as having been made on the last day of the tax year.
13. See, e.g., *Steel Balls, Inc. v. Commissioner,* T.C. Memo 1995-266, 19 EBC 1583, aff'd 96-1 USTC 50,309 (8th Cir. 1996).
14. The Internal Revenue Code does not treat most S corporation distributions as "dividends" for tax law purposes, since most S corporations do not have "earnings and profits," but the term "dividends" is still used in this paragraph for simplicity and because under state law these amounts are still dividends.
15. PLR 199938052 (July 2, 1999).
16. P.L. 108-357, § 240.

Chapter 3

Section 1042 and the Tax-Deferred ESOP "Rollover"

Scott S. Rodrick

One of the main uses of a leveraged ESOP is to buy out the owner or owners of a closely held company. An ESOP is ideally suited to that task for various reasons: for example, it provides a ready market for the selling owner's shares; an owner or owners can sell in stages instead of all at once; it preserves continuity at the company by not bringing in a third-party buyer who may disrupt operations (e.g., by firing people or selling off parts of the company); employees are given a new retirement plan that, in conjunction with a participative management approach, can produce notable performance gains; and the company receives tax deductions for its contributions to the ESOP.

But there is yet another factor that drives many leveraged ESOP transactions: the tax-deferred "ESOP rollover." Under Internal Revenue Code ("Code") Section 1042, the owner(s) of a closely held C corporation can indefinitely postpone taxation on the gain resulting from the ESOP sale to the extent they reinvest ("roll over") the sale proceeds in securities of U.S. operating corporations. Nobody likes to pay taxes, even at the lower long-term capital gains rates enacted in 2002 (15% for those in the upper tax brackets), and the savings afforded by the "ESOP rollover" are a powerful incentive for prospective sellers to an ESOP.[1]

The Section 1042 Rules in Brief

Section 1042 was not originally part of ESOP law. It was added to the Internal Revenue Code by the Tax Reform Act of 1984.[2] It does not apply automatically; rather, the selling owner must affirmatively elect Section 1042 treatment.

This chapter will begin with a brief summary of the rules for the tax deferral and then follow with a more detailed discussion of each point. Most of these rules are contained in Section 1042 and other sections of the Code, but others are in temporary regulations promulgated by the Internal Revenue Service (IRS) in 1986. Also note that not all of these rules apply to the seller. Namely, violating the requirements for the ESOP to avoid allocating stock from the 1042 transaction to certain individuals and to avoid disposing of the stock within three years results in excise taxes to the company, but such prohibited allocations and prohibited dispositions of the stock do not disqualify the tax deferral for the shareholder(s) who sold to the ESOP in the transaction.

- The company sponsoring the ESOP must be a closely held C corporation, not a publicly traded company or an S corporation.
- The ESOP must own at least 30% of the common equity of the company after the transaction.
- The selling shareholder cannot be a C or S corporation but rather must be an individual, trust, estate, or partnership.
- The stock sold to the ESOP must have been held by the seller for at least three years before the sale. (When stock ownership is exchanged for a prior partnership or LLC interest, the total time of ownership is measured, as described below.)
- The stock sold to the ESOP must *not* have been acquired through a qualified retirement plan (such as an ESOP) or through a stock option or other discounted employee stock purchase arrangement.
- The stock sold to the ESOP must be common stock with certain voting power and dividend rights, or preferred stock convertible into such common stock.
- During a period starting three months before the sale and ending a year after the sale, the seller must reinvest ("roll over") the proceeds or an equivalent sum of money (in any amount up to the amount of the sale) in "qualified replacement property" (QRP) (basically, the securities of U.S. operating companies).
- With certain exceptions, if the ESOP disposes of any of the stock within three years after the sale, the company must pay a 10% excise tax.

Section 1042 and the Tax-Deferred ESOP "Rollover" 43

- For at least ten years after the sale, the ESOP must not allocate stock bought in the sale to the ESOP accounts of the seller or certain relatives of the seller; with no time limitation, the ESOP must not allocate such stock to any more-than-25% shareholders or to related parties of more-than-25% shareholders deemed to hold stock by attribution. Otherwise, the company must pay a 50% excise tax, and the person receiving the allocation is currently taxable on the value of the allocation.
- After the sale, the seller must file the following two documents with the seller's income tax return for the year in which the sale occurs:
    1. A "statement of election" under which the seller elects tax-deferred treatment.
    2. A verified statement from the company consenting to the imposition of the 10% and 50% excise taxes referred to above if the ESOP disposes of the stock within three years after the sale or makes a prohibited allocation.

    Furthermore, every time the seller purchases QRP, the seller must obtain:
3. A notarized "statement of purchase," which then must be filed as discussed below. (If the QRP has been bought at the time of the Section 1042 election, the statement(s) of purchase must be filed along with the statement of election.)

The Section 1042 Rules in Detail

Nature of the ESOP Sponsor

Section 1042 applies only to sales to an ESOP established in a domestic C corporation.[3] For at least one year before and immediately after the sale, the company, and each corporation that is a member of a "controlled group of corporations" with the company, must have no stock outstanding that is readily tradable on an established securities market.[4]

S corporations formerly could not even have an ESOP that held company stock; now (since January 1997) they can, but selling shareholders cannot take advantage of Section 1042. An S corporation that wishes to make the Section 1042 "rollover" available to its shareholders may terminate its S corporation election, thus converting to C status.[5] A company wishing to elect S status may stay a C corporation long enough for the tax-deferred sale to the ESOP to take place, and then elect S status the year after the sale.

The 30% Requirement

Immediately after the sale, the ESOP must own at least 30% of either each class of outstanding stock or the total value of all outstanding stock (excluding nonconvertible, nonvoting preferred stock).[6] Note that the ESOP need not own any stock before the sale.

Sales to the ESOP by two or more owners can be treated as a single sale meeting the 30% requirement if they are "part of a single, integrated transaction under a prearranged agreement" between the sellers.[7]

Who the Selling Shareholder Can Be

Usually, the selling shareholders who elect Section 1042 are individuals. They also can be partnerships, trusts, estates, or limited liability companies (LLCs). They cannot, however, be C or S corporations.[8] If the seller is a partnership or LLC, it is the partnership or LLC itself, not individual partners or members, that makes the Section 1042 election and purchases the QRP.[9]

Nature of the Stock Sold in a 1042 Transaction

The stock sold to the ESOP must have been held by the seller for at least three years before the ESOP transaction, determined as of the time of the sale.[10]

To reach the three-year holding requirement, a seller who has held the stock for less than three years may take advantage of the "tacking" rules in Section 1223 of the Code. These rules allow the seller, in certain circumstances, to "tack" on the holding period of an asset that was exchanged for the stock in a transaction where both the stock and the asset for which it was exchanged has the same basis (i.e., a gift or tax-free exchange).[11]

The gain on the sale of stock sold to the ESOP must be otherwise eligible for long-term capital gain treatment, i.e., it cannot be stock that is ineligible for capital gain treatment, such as preferred stock subject to Code Section 306.

The stock sold to the ESOP must not have been acquired through a qualified retirement plan (such as an ESOP) or through a stock option or other employee stock purchase arrangement.[12]

The stock sold to the ESOP must be (1) common stock having a combination of voting power and dividend rights equal to or in excess of (a) the class of common stock having the greatest voting power and (b) the class of common stock having the greatest dividend rights, or (2) preferred stock convertible into such common stock at a reasonable conversion price.[13] (Note: this is not a Section 1042 requirement but rather is a general requirement for most ESOP tax incentives applicable to closely held companies.)

Qualified Replacement Property (QRP)

To obtain the Section 1042 tax deferral, the seller must reinvest proceeds of the sale in QRP during a period beginning 3 months before and ending 12 months after the date of the sale, i.e., the date the stock is sold to the ESOP.[14] The tax deferral lasts as long as the seller holds the QRP (this is discussed more below).

The IRS does not trace the funds from the sale; as is apparent from the "3 months before" aspect of this rule, the actual funds from the sale need not be used. For example, a seller who has $1 million dollars to invest can buy QRP three months before the ESOP transaction, receive $1 million in the transaction, and freely invest or spend the $1 million in proceeds from the actual sale.

Also note that the seller can elect Section 1042 treatment for any amount of the sale proceeds. Of course, this means that the seller will pay capital gains taxes on the amount not reinvested under Section 1042. Thus, a selling shareholder might receive $1 million from an ESOP transaction, reinvest half of it in QRP and elect Section 1042 treatment for that amount, and spend the other half (or rather what remains of it after paying capital gains taxes) on a new house.

The QRP itself must consist of stocks or bonds issued by a domestic operating corporation. A domestic corporation is one incorporated in the U.S. Section 1042 defines an "operating corporation" as one where more than 50% of the company's assets were used in the active conduct of a business as of the time the security was purchased or before the end of the 15-month period for buying QRP. No more than 25% of the corporation's gross income can come from passive investment income.[15] However, shares in certain financial institutions and in insurance companies subject to taxation are excluded from the passive income rule and thus can constitute QRP.[16] Government securities cannot be QRP.[17]

The rollover securities need to qualify as QRP only when the seller buys them and elects to treat them as QRP. If, for example, a seller buys a company's stock as QRP and a few years later the company becomes a non-operating company or reincorporates in a foreign country, the seller can keep holding the stock as QRP.

The QRP must consist of the actual securities themselves, not mutual funds. Real estate investment trusts (REITs) and partnership interests also are off-limits.

There is no prohibition against reinvesting in securities of closely held companies, but the QRP cannot include securities of the ESOP company itself—that is, the company whose shares were sold to the ESOP (i.e., a shareholder in Company X cannot sell 30% of Company X's stock to Company X's new ESOP and then buy more Company X stock to serve as QRP). Corporations controlled by the ESOP company or that own stock representing control of the ESOP company are also excluded from being QRP.[18] However, it would be permissible for the QRP to consist of shares in another company owned by the seller that was not in the same controlled group of corporations, including a new corporation funded wholly with the ESOP sale proceeds.[19]

Investment advisors who specialize in assisting clients who sell to an ESOP develop various strategies to maximize the benefits of Section 1042. For example, one commonly discussed strategy is the use of what are sometimes called "ESOP Notes"—long-term corporate bonds designed to serve as an ESOP rollover investment. These are floating-rate notes that combine a long maturity (such as 60 years) with call protection for a lengthy period (such as 30 years), which means that they can be held for a long time without being called (which would constitute a disposition of the QRP, which in turn would trigger the capital gains taxes that the QRP investment was intended to delay in the first place). The selling shareholder may be able to borrow up to 75% or more of the value of the floating-rate note and invest the borrowed sums freely while still deferring taxes on the original sale to the ESOP, which has considerable appeal for some individuals. However, the income from the floating-rate note often will not even pay all the interest due on the borrowed money, so to profit from this strategy, the shareholder must (after any brokerage and management fees) generate higher returns with the 75% or so that was borrowed than he or she would with 100% of the sale proceeds invested in a conventional buy-and-hold QRP portfolio. Accordingly, the floating-rate note QRP strategy may be best suited for younger, aggressive investors who expect that over time, the growth of their actively managed portfolio will surpass that of a passive buy-and-hold QRP investment.

Another interesting technique is to have the selling shareholder donate some of all of the sale proceeds to a charitable remainder trust. In return, the shareholder receives a tax deduction plus annual income for the remainder of the shareholder's life, for the lives of the shareholder and his or her spouse, or for a fixed period. The gift is irrevocable, however, and thus the shareholder's heirs will not inherit the sale proceeds.

Selling shareholders should not feel compelled to follow the kinds of special investment strategies outlined above. In many cases, they and their advisors will conclude that the best strategy for them is simply to invest in stocks and bonds that qualify as QRP and that would be good long-term investments regardless of their status as QRP.[20]

As noted above, when the seller disposes of any QRP, the gain that was deferred is now realized, and the seller must pay taxes on the portion of the deferred gain that the sale represents.[21] The basis of the QRP is the basis of the stock sold to the ESOP.[22] However, no gain is realized if the stock is exchanged for stock of another company in a tax-free corporate reorganization under Code Section 368, by reason of the seller's death, by gift (such as a charitable contribution, or a transfer to a charitable remainder trust or to the seller's relatives), or in another transaction to which Section 1042 applies.[23] And if a seller holds QRP when he or she dies, the heirs receive a basis in the QRP that is stepped-up to the fair market value of the stock at the time of death,[24] thus achieving a complete avoidance of taxation on the proceeds of the sale to the ESOP.

Some sellers have the misconception that holding QRP is like holding stock in a tax-deferred account such as an IRA, where dividends and interest on the assets held in the account are not taxable. This is not the case with QRP: the tax deferral applies only to the proceeds from the sale to the ESOP, and all earnings from the QRP are taxed.

The ESOP's Three-Year Holding Period

If the ESOP disposes of any stock within three years after the sale, the company must pay a 10% excise tax on the amount realized by the ESOP on the disposition. The IRS does not trace the particular shares that were sold. Rather, the Code imposes the tax if, after the disposition in question, either (1) the total number of shares in the ESOP is now less than the total number that the ESOP held immediately after the sale, or (2) the value of the stock held by the ESOP is now less than 30% of the value of all employer securities as of the date of the disposition.[25]

The foregoing rule does not apply to an exchange of stock by the ESOP for stock of another corporation in certain tax-free reorganizations, or to benefit distributions due to termination of employment or in connection with ESOP diversification requirements.[26]

The Prohibited Allocation Rule

If the selling shareholder elects the Section 1042 tax deferral, the ESOP is prohibited from making allocations of stock from that transaction to the seller, more-than-25% shareholders, and certain relatives.

For the later of 10 years after the sale or after the final allocation of stock attributable to the sale if it was a leveraged transaction, the ESOP cannot make allocations of stock from the 1042 transaction to the selling shareholder and anyone related to the seller as defined by Code Section 267(b).[27] Such relatives include, for example, siblings, spouses, ancestors, lineal descendants (including legally adopted children), and partners (where the selling shareholder is a partnership), but do *not* include aunts and uncles, nieces and nephews, stepchildren and stepparents, and in-laws.[28]

So long as shares from the 1042 transaction remain in the ESOP, they cannot be allocated to more-than-25% shareholders. More than 25% means not just more than 25% of the entire company but also more than 25% of any class of stock, more than 25% of the value of any class of stock, or more than 25% of any class of stock (or the value of such stock) in a member of the same controlled group of corporations.[29] For purposes of determining the percentage of ownership, one must include stock owned by certain other parties, which include, for example, spouses, children (including legally adopted children), grandchildren, and parents; additionally, stock allocated to the individual under the ESOP must be counted. The parties whose ownership interests are included do *not* include grandparents, stepchildren and stepparents, siblings, aunts and uncles, nieces and nephews, cousins, and in-laws.[30]

It is important to note that under the attribution rules, someone may be a more-than-25% shareholder even if they are not usually thought of as being a shareholder at all. Thus, if someone owns 30% of the company, a son of that owner who works for the company will also be considered a more-than-25% shareholder and thus prohibited from receiving ESOP allocations of stock sold in the Section 1042 transaction. The more-than-25% ownership test is applied to the entire one-year period ending with the date of sale to the ESOP, and also on the date that stock sold in the 1042 sale is allocated to ESOP participants.[31]

There is an exception to the prohibited allocation rule: a total of 5% of the stock sold in the Section 1042 transaction can be allocated to a seller's lineal descendants.[32] There is no equivalent exception for lineal descendants who are considered more-than-25% shareholders by attribution. Indeed, the IRS has ruled that regardless of the 5% exception, the seller's lineal descendants are still prohibited from receiving allocations if they are more-than-25% shareholders by attribution. This essentially cancels out the lineal descendant exception for many people: since the more-than-25% test is applied to the entire year before the sale, even the lineal descendants of an owner who owns less than 25% after the 1042 transaction will be considered more-than-25% owners for purposes of this test if the owner had more than 25% during the year before the sale. Thus, the lineal descendant exception is very narrow, applying only where the seller held less than 25% of any class of stock during the year preceding the sale (i.e., where the ESOP already held some stock or where the seller aggregated his or her shares with another seller's shares to reach the 30% threshold for Section 1042).

If the prohibited allocation rule is violated, the company sponsoring the ESOP must pay a 50% excise tax on the amount involved, and the person receiving the allocation is currently taxable on the value of the allocation.[33]

If the company wishes to compensate key employees who are prohibited from receiving ESOP allocations under the above rules, it cannot use a tax-qualified retirement plan meeting the requirements of Code Section 401(a) to allocate shares in place of the prohibited ESOP shares.[34] Instead, the company must use plans such as stock options (including tax-qualified options), restricted stock, phantom stock, stock appreciation rights (SARs), and direct stock purchases.[35]

Procedural Requirements for the Selling Shareholder

The selling shareholder cannot simply sell to an ESOP and reinvest the proceeds in QRP without further ado. Rather, the seller must affirmatively elect Section 1042 treatment in a "statement of election" attached to the seller's income tax return for the taxable year in which the sale occurs, filed on or before the due date (including extensions of time). The 1042 election cannot be revoked once it has been made.[36] The statement of election must describe the securities sold to the ESOP, the date of the sale, the adjusted basis of the securities and the amount realized on the sale, the identity of the ESOP, and, if the sale was part of a single transaction involving other sellers, their names and taxpayer identification numbers and the number of shares they sold.[37]

For each purchase of QRP (which itself can take place only within the 15-month window of opportunity described above), the seller must execute and have notarized a "statement of purchase" declaring it to be QRP, describing it, and noting its cost and date of purchase. Under temporary regulations issued in 1986, the statement of purchase has had to be notarized within 30 days after the purchase of QRP.[38] This 30-day requirement has led to many inadvertent errors by taxpayers, and so the IRS is liberalizing the filing requirement. In July 2003, the IRS proposed amending the temporary regulations to allow the statement of purchase to be notarized any time not later than the filing of the seller's tax return for the year in which the 1042 sale occurred, or, if the QRP was purchased after that (but within the allowed period), any time not later than the filing of the seller's tax return for the year following the year in which the Section 1042 election was made. The IRS's notice states that, pending the issuance of final regulations, taxpayers may begin relying on the new rule for all open taxable years.[39]

If the seller has already bought the QRP at the time of the 1042 election, the statement of purchase must be attached as part of the statement of election that is filed with the seller's tax return. Otherwise, the statement of purchase must be attached to the seller's income tax return for the year following the year in which the seller elected 1042 treatment.[40]

Finally, the seller must file with the statement of election a verified statement of consent from the corporation consenting to the imposition of excise taxes on the corporation under Code Sections 4978 (i.e., a 10% tax if the ESOP disposes of the shares from the Section 1042 sale within three years) and 4979A (i.e., a 50% tax if a prohibited allocation is made).[41]

The IRS does not provide official forms for the statement of election, statement of purchase, or statement of consent; taxpayers and practitioners simply read the statute and regulations and follow the rather straightforward requirements set forth there.[42]

The IRS has stated that failure to comply with procedural requirements for the Section 1042 election is not necessarily fatal where such requirements appear only in the IRS's regulations and do not go to the essence of the statute. Thus, where sellers have failed to obtain statements of purchase within 30 days of buying QRP (a purely regulatory requirement, which the IRS is now in the process of modifying as noted above), the IRS has often ruled that the sellers "substantially complied" with the regulations in those particular circumstances (for example, where the seller had immediately completed a notarized statement of purchase upon learning of the requirement for one, had filed a private letter ruling request, and/or had relied on tax professionals to prepare any necessary forms).[43] The IRS has also applied this logic in a broader context, as when it ruled that a seller substantially complied with the requirements under Section 1042 where the seller failed to file the statement of election, statement of purchase, and statement of consent with his tax return, but then discovered these requirements and filed an amended return that incorporated these forms.[44] Please note that one is not automatically excused from complying with the Section 1042 requirements in circumstances such as the above, but rather must receive a specific ruling from the IRS pertaining to one's own situation.

Special Situations

There are situations in which company owners would ordinarily not seem eligible for the Section 1042 "rollover," at least not completely, but in which proper transaction structuring can result in a complete tax deferral under Section 1042.

How to Use Seller Financing and Yet Elect Section 1042 Treatment on All the Proceeds

Sometimes sellers finance the ESOP transaction themselves by receiving a note from the ESOP for some or all of the sale price. They may do this because bank financing is too expensive or difficult to obtain, because the company is subject to bonding and the bonding agency views an ESOP loan as excessive leverage, or for other reasons.

As noted above, the election to defer capital gains taxes under Section 1042 is effective only for the portion of the sale proceeds that is reinvested during the period from 3 months before to 12 months after the sale to the ESOP. This raises a problem for sellers who are financing the sale: If they have no other funds (that is, other than the proceeds from the sale to the ESOP) to invest in QRP, then some of the sale proceeds will likely be paid to them after the 15-month reinvestment period, and they will have to pay capital gains taxes on a portion of the proceeds. The fact that they are receiving the funds years after the sale does not alter this rule.[45]

There is a way out of this dilemma, however: the seller can use "leveraged QRP"—that is, borrow the funds to reinvest in QRP within the 15-month reinvestment period. One method is to have the QRP serve as collateral for the loan that supplies the funds to purchase it. Investment advisors who have developed this technique use the floating-rate notes mentioned above under the heading "Qualified Replacement Property (QRP)." The seller can use the installment payments from the ESOP (and/or income from the QRP) to pay down the loan taken out to buy the QRP.[46]

How People Who Sell to *Another* Company's ESOP Can Elect Section 1042 Treatment

The most common ESOP issue in mergers and acquisitions is how the owner of a non-ESOP company being acquired by an ESOP company can elect the Section 1042 tax deferral for the proceeds of the sale. It is not feasible to have the seller sell to his or her own ESOP and then sell the company to the acquiring company. It is, however, possible to use other methods, such as a reverse merger, in which the acquiring company is merged into the target company, after which the owner of the target company can sell to the ESOP. (Keep in mind that no matter what method is used, the seller must meet the usual Section 1042 requirements described above.)

Regulations published by the IRS in 1998 would seem to make a straightforward acquisition allowable: here, the target company merges into the acquirer, the target company's owner receives shares in the acquirer in exchange for his or her ownership interest in the target company, and the target company's owner then sells those shares to the acquirer's ESOP. However, the regulations deal with "continuity of interest" rules in general, not with ESOPs, and it is not certain at this time that the IRS would approve this approach. The chapter in this book on "ESOPs in Mergers and Acquisitions" discusses this topic in detail.

Conclusion

The tax deferral under Section 1042 helps make a leveraged sale to an ESOP the ideal business succession strategy for many owners of closely held companies. It allows the company to simultaneously defer or eliminate the taxation of the proceeds of the owner's sale of his or her shares while creating an ownership plan for the company's employees. The rules for Section 1042 are many and sometimes complex, but, as with other aspects of ESOPs, careful planning with competent legal counsel can smooth over bumps encountered on the road to employee ownership.

Notes

1. The tax-deferred "ESOP rollover" for the seller under Section 1042 should not be confused with the tax-free rollover of an ESOP distribution into an ESOP participant's IRA or other qualified benefit plan.
2. Section 1042 applies not only to ESOPs but also to certain worker-owned cooperatives. This discussion will focus on ESOPs because this book is about ESOPs. Additionally, Section 1042 is almost always used for ESOPs.
3. Code § 1042(c)(1)(A).
4. Ibid.; Temp. Treas. Reg. § 1.1042-1T, Q&A-1(b).
5. No delay is needed after termination of the S election. In PLR 200003014 (Oct. 20, 1999), the IRS ruled that a seller could undertake a Section 1042

sale immediately after the company changed from a S corporation to a C corporation.

6. Code § 1042(b)(2).
7. Temp. Treas. Reg. § 1.1042-1T, Q&A-2(b).
8. Code § 1042(c)(7) (regarding C corporations). Section 1042 does not specifically exclude S corporations from acting as selling shareholders in this context. However, in 2001, during discussions leading to an ESOP-related private letter ruling, the IRS firmly rejected a suggestion by the ESOP practitioners requesting the PLR that an S corporation could sell to an ESOP and elect tax-deferred 1042 treatment. The practitioners then withdrew that issue from their PLR request.
9. Technical Advice Memorandum 9508001 (October 13, 1994) and PLR 9846005 (November 13, 1998) (dealing with partnerships); PLR 200243001 (October 25, 2002) (dealing with an LLC). Note: for federal tax purposes, an LLC is generally treated as a partnership.
10. Code § 1042(b)(4).
11. Douglas Jaques, "'Tacking' On to the Section 1042 Seller's Holding Period," in *Selling to an ESOP*, 8th ed. (Oakland, CA: NCEO, 2005).
12. Code § 1042(c)(1)(B). Although the statute is unclear on this point, many ESOP practitioners think that stock acquired at fair market value (or above) in an employee stock purchase arrangement should be eligible for Section 1042 sales. However, at least one IRS representative has informally stated that this is not that case and that absolutely no stock acquired through an employee stock purchase arrangement may be sold to an ESOP in a Section 1042 transaction.
13. Code §§ 1042(c)(1), 409(l).
14. Code § 1042(c)(3).
15. Code § 1042(c)(4)(A)-(B).
16. Code § 1042(c)(4)(B)(ii).
17. Code § 1042(c)(4)(D).
18. Code § 1042(c)(4)(C).
19. PLR 9720026 (Feb. 12, 1997).
20. See James H. Willis and Michael A. Coffey, "Reinvesting the Section 1042 Rollover," in *Selling to an ESOP*, which discusses floating-rate notes, charitable remainder trusts, and other strategies and general considerations.
21. Code § 1042(e)(1).
22. Code § 1042(d). Literally, the taxpayer's basis in the QRP is reduced by the gain not recognized due to the 1042 election, so the basis of the stock sold to the ESOP becomes the basis of the QRP. This means that if the QRP loses value and is sold, the seller may still owe taxes. For example, say that the

owner's basis in the stock is $200,000, and he sells it to the ESOP for its fair market value of $1 million. To avoid paying taxes on the $800,000 gain, he reinvests the $1 million in 10 stocks at $100,000 each and elects Section 1042 treatment. Under Code Section 1042(d), the unrecognized gain of $800,000 reduces his $1 million basis in the QRP to the $200,000 level of the stock sold to the ESOP, allocated pro-rata to each of the investments. Years later, the value of one of the $100,000 QRP investments has fallen to $50,000, and the seller disposes of the stock. Although he lost half of his $100,000 investment in this portion of the QRP, its basis is $20,000 (i.e., its pro-rata portion of the $200,000 basis in the stock sold to the ESOP), and he now owes taxes on $30,000 (the difference between the $50,000 in proceeds from the sale of the QRP and the $20,000 basis of the QRP).

23. Code § 1042(e)(3).
24. Code § 1014.
25. Code § 4978(a)-(b).
26. Code § 4978(d). To be precise, Section 4978(d) refers not to termination in general but specifically to distributions due to death, disability, retirement after age 59½, and separation from service resulting in a one-year break in service.
27. Code § 409(n)(1)(A) and (3)(C). When multiple sellers elect Section 1042 treatment, none of them can receive allocations of stock from the other sellers' ESOP transactions. See Code Section 409(n)(1)(A)(i) and PLR 9041071 (Oct. 12, 1990).
28. Brian B. Snarr, "The Prohibited Allocation Rule Under Section 1042," in *Selling to an ESOP*, text under the heading "Certain Relatives of the Selling Shareholder" (summarizing Section 267's provisions and other authorities).
29. Code § 409(n)(1)(B).
30. Brian B. Snarr, "The Prohibited Allocation Rule Under Section 1042," text under the heading "More-Than-25% Shareholders" (summarizing Section 318's provisions and other authorities).
31. Code § 409(n)(3)(B).
32. Code § 409(n)(3)(A).
33. Code § 7979A.
34. Code § 409(n)(1).
35. These plans are described in NCEO books such as *The Stock Options Book* and *Beyond Stock Options*.
36. Code § 1042(a)(1), (c)(6); Temp. Treas. Reg. § 1.1042-1T, Q&A-3(a).
37. Temp. Treas. Reg. § 1.1042-1T, Q&A-3(b).
38. Ibid.
39. REG-121122-03, Internal Revenue Bulletin 2003-37 (July 10, 2003).

40. Temp. Treas. Reg. § 1.1042-1T, Q&A-3(b)-(c).
41. Code §§ 1042(b)(3), 4978(a)-(b), 4979A; Temp. Treas. Reg. § 1.1042-1T, Q&A-2(a)(4), Q&A-3(b).
42. Sample forms are provided as appendices to Willis and Coffey, "Reinvesting the Section 1042 Rollover" (a statement of election, statement of purchase, and statement of consent).
43. See, e.g., PLR 9821022 (Feb. 17, 1998), PLR 9846015 (Aug. 13, 1998), and PLR 9852004 (Sept. 16, 1998).
44. PLR 9619065 (May 10, 1996). However, compare *Estate of Clause v. Comm.*, 122 T.C. No. 5 (Feb. 9, 2004), in which the U.S. Tax Court held the petitioner, who sold stock to an ESOP in 1996 and purchased QRP within one year of the sale but failed to report it in any way on his tax return for 1996, could not defer recognition of tax under Section 1042 because he failed to file a timely 1042 election and thus failed to elect 1042 treatment. The petitioner in *Clause* filed amended returns (with a statement of election of Section 1042 treatment, a statement of consent from the company, and a statement of purchase of QRP) in 2001, after the IRS had commenced an audit of his 1996 return and mailed the petitioner a notice of deficiency for 1996, but to no avail.
45. PLR 8644024 (Aug. 1, 1986).
46. See Bruce F. Bickley and James G. Steiker, "Seller-Financed ESOPs and Leveraged QRP Transactions," in *Selling to an ESOP*, which explores this topic in detail.

Chapter 4

Financing the Leveraged ESOP

Kenneth E. Serwinski

Borrowing money to finance a leveraged employee stock ownership plan (ESOP) can be a challenge for closely held companies. Most successful business owners have learned that debt management over a long period of time can be quite demanding. Financing a leveraged ESOP actually recapitalizes the company, which is necessary to fund this exit strategy for existing shareholders. The bottom line is that the business owners are replacing equity with nonproductive debt. The strategy behind structuring a good transaction is to minimize the effects on the balance sheet and cash flows so ongoing working capital and capital expenditure needs are not inhibited. Before considering structuring issues, one should understand some of the credit criteria necessary to obtain this type of loan.

The Four C's of Lending

When deciding whether to grant a loan, lenders often base their decision on what are commonly known as the four C's of lending: character, cash flow, collateral, and capital.

Character

In evaluating an ESOP's feasibility in a closely held business, an honest assessment of the existing management is necessary. The success of an ESOP will be determined by management's ability to create a culture that will allow the new ESOP company to thrive. Inexperienced management could hinder the establishment of a successful ESOP.

When reviewing a phased ESOP transaction, one must consider the expected future involvement of the current business owner. In a phased ESOP transaction, the owner remains involved while creating an employee ownership environment and discovering new managerial talent. Many companies establish an ESOP to give quality management personnel the opportunity to demonstrate themselves as the owner's true successor. As a control transaction occurs, the lender places greater emphasis on the depth of management than on the involvement of the former owner.

Finally, lenders look to the credit history of both the owner and the company to understand the true character of each. A poor credit payment history, combined with litigation problems, would certainly turn off most lenders.

Cash Flow

Most successful ESOPs result from successful companies. To analyze the effects of an ESOP loan on the company, advisors tend to look for good historical trends of profitability and cash flow. More importantly, one should study realistic projections of the company and its profitability during the course of the loan's amortization period. Projections can be difficult to rely upon; however, most companies can project the next two years' performance with some reliability. Because the ESOP loan, which represents nonproductive debt, is being put in place, the debt service coverage that most lenders look for would be in the range of 1.25 to 1.75 times cash flow. This is an indicative range. Some aggressive lenders may agree to a lower multiple for the first two years of the loan and establish a provision for a larger cushion over time.

Last but not least, because this is nonproductive debt, the company needs to satisfy its ongoing working capital and capital expenditure requirements. Thus, the company must have access to further credit if it cannot finance growth internally. The key is to structure a deal that will allow the company to continue to grow despite the addition of ESOP debt. The combination of understanding historical trends and future projections, along with adequate debt service coverage and access to additional credit, are important factors in structuring an ESOP loan that will not "kill" the company.

Collateral

The company generally must make collateral available for any loan it makes, including an ESOP loan. The lender, which always requires a second "way out" of a loan, will liquidate this collateral if chronic cash flow shortfalls occur. Once the collateral is known, its strength must be determined. Most businesses in a manufacturing environment have accounts receivable, inventory, equipment, and real estate available as collateral. Some of those assets, however, may already be used as collateral for the working capital, lines of credit, equipment loans, or real estate mortgages. If, however, some of the longer-term assets, such as equipment and real estate, are unencumbered, such assets might make reasonable forms of collateral to many lenders. Ideally, long-term loans should always be collateralized with these fixed assets.

If, as in the case of service businesses, there are limited fixed assets available for collateral, other alternatives may need to be considered. The most prominent alternative in service businesses is the pledging of Section 1042 replacement securities. (Section 1042 of the Internal Revenue Code allows the owner of a closely held C corporation to defer taxation of gains on stock he or she sells to an ESOP if the ESOP owns 30% of the company's stock after the sale and the selling shareholder reinvests, or "rolls over," the proceeds in qualifying replacement securities.)

Capital

After addressing whether the company has enough management infrastructure to make an ESOP loan work, whether the company has enough cash flow to handle the debt, and whether the lender feels comfortable with the collateral available, the next task is to understand the company's capital base. Adding an ESOP term loan will significantly affect the company's balance sheet and leverage, as tables 4-1 and 4-2 below illustrate. Table 4-1 demonstrates that the company has total liabilities of $8 million against a net worth of $6 million, producing a leverage ratio of 1.33 to 1.

After the $3 million ESOP loan is implemented, the total liabilities increase to $11 million, and there is a contra hit to equity of a similar dollar amount increasing the leverage from 1.33 to 1 to 3.67 to 1 (table 4-2).

ESOP Loan Structure

From the previous discussion, one can understand that structuring an ESOP loan can be quite challenging. Not only is the impact of the

TABLE 4-1. Balance Sheet Before Stock Purchase ($3,000,000 loan to buy 33% of outstanding shares).

Current Assets	$ 8,000,000	Current Liabilities	$5,000,000
Fixed Assets	6,000,000	Long-Term Liabilities	3,000,000
Total Assets	$14,000,000	Total Liabilities	$8,000,000
		Net Worth (Assets – Liabilities)	$6,000,000
		Leveraged Ratio	1.33 to 1

TABLE 4-2. Balance Sheet After Stock Purchase ($3,000,000 loan to buy 33% of outstanding shares).

Current Assets	$ 8,000,000	Current Liabilities	$ 5,000,000
Fixed Assets	6,000,000	ESOP Loan	3,000,000
Total Assets	$14,000,000	Long-Term Liabilities	3,000,000
		Total Liabilities	$11,000,000
		Net Worth (Assets – Liabilities)	$ 3,000,000
		Leveraged Ratio	3.67 to 1

ESOP loan an issue; one must also be concerned with future working capital and capital expenditure needs so as not to encumber the company in such a manner that future growth is prohibited. ESOP loans are usually structured as follows:

Loan A loan can be made either to the company or to the ESOP trust. Most lenders prefer to make ESOP loans to the company, since the loan then becomes a direct obligation of the company. The company in turn will make a mirror loan at substantially the same terms and conditions to the ESOP trust. A minority of lenders would consider loaning directly to the ESOP trust, but only if the company guaranteed the loan.

Amortization ESOP loans typically have amortization periods of from five to ten years, with five- to seven-year full payout terms being the most popular. Most lenders are quite reluctant to go longer than ten years, and even then there will probably be a balloon payment after year five and certainly after year seven.

Collateral Lenders may ask for collateral that ranges from Section 1042 replacement securities to receivables, inventory, equipment, and real estate.

Covenants The imposition of covenants is directly related to the level of debt inside the company. It is not unusual, however, for lenders to have covenants for minimum cash flow coverage or debt service along with covenants for net worth to be kept at certain levels. Additionally, restrictions may be placed on dividend payments, amounts of capital expenditures, and bonus and compensation limits for existing shareholders.

Guarantees Selling shareholders often must give personal guarantees, which can be a sticking point for them. The quality of collateral and the level of cash flow may determine whether and to what degree personal guarantees are necessary. Some guarantees cover collateral shortfalls. For example, if a borrower seeks a $2 million ESOP loan and the bank, understanding the liquidation value of the assets being pledged, finds that the borrower is a half million dollars short in collateral, the bank will require a limited guarantee only up to that half million dollars. When Section 1042 rollover securities are pledged, the quality of the collateral is such that some lenders will forgo the personal guarantee to obtain 100% liquid collateral.

What the Lender Will Ask For

Ideally, the lender, in considering the proposal for an ESOP loan, will look for at least three to five years of historical financial information. Financial statements must, at a minimum, be reviewed; preferably, they should be audited. In addition to financial statements, the lender will look for pro forma projections for both the income statement and the balance sheet. Providing the projections is just the beginning. Notes to those projections should include the assumptions underlying them. For example, where improvements in operating margins that have not occurred in the past are projected into the future, the reason for the improvement must be revealed. These pro forma projections must also include potential cost reductions, which can occur in many ways. Perhaps the selling shareholder is willing to reduce his or her salary to enhance the cash flow position.

Alternatively, the company and its employees may decide to freeze or cut back wages to make the ESOP work.

Finally, the lender will ask for a report on available collateral. This will include an accounts receivable aging; an inventory breakdown, if appropriate, between raw materials, work in process and finished goods inventory; a fixed assets schedule; and appraisals of fixed assets as well as of the availability of the Section 1042 rollover securities as collateral.

The Borrower's Perspective

Although we have been reviewing what a lender might consider important in making an ESOP loan, it is appropriate to consider the borrower's perspective as well. ESOP financing has significant advantages over traditional forms of debt. The owner has probably looked at other exit strategies and determined that they are not appropriate for his or her particular company. There are few exit strategies available to the business owner, namely:

- *An initial public offering.* Taking the company public is not a complete exit strategy for the business owner. It can, however, be a phased exit strategy for the right kind of business.

- *Selling the business outright.* Selling the business to a third party is a definite consideration for many business owners. However, most buyers of a business do not pay completely in cash. They may pay a significant portion of the price, somewhere between 40% to 70%, as a down payment, but some form of seller financing may be required. Thus, the business owner becomes a partner with a buyer he or she does not really know.

- *Recapitalization for a family or management buyout.* To fund a family or management buyout, a significant amount of debt, either senior debt or senior/subordinated debt, may be required to effect a transfer of ownership. This can incur significant levels of debt, with the amortization of the loans being made with after-tax dollars.

- *Recapitalization using an ESOP.* This is a tax-advantaged form of recapitalizing the business for shareholders to realize value and liquidity. Because the ESOP is a qualified retirement plan, the company can make contributions to the ESOP on a pretax basis. This feature allows for amortizing the ESOP loan, both principal and interest, on a tax-deductible basis.

What Should the Borrowers Look For?

Borrowers must find lenders experienced in ESOP financing. Lenders inexperienced with ESOPs need a tremendous amount of "hand holding" to effect the transaction. When evaluating proposals from lenders, terms and conditions play a significant role. Look for favorable terms in amortization schedules, collateral, and guarantees. Rates and fees are certainly important, but realize that the lender is actually being asked to finance a leveraged buyout of existing shareholders and that rates and fees may reflect that level of risk.

Alternatives

As a general rule, owners of closely held businesses shy away from leveraging up the balance sheet of their company. Thus, the idea of a leveraged ESOP scares them. There may be other alternatives that still allow owners to consider a leveraged ESOP. Some companies have significant amounts of corporate cash or marketable securities. Such a company can self-finance a leveraged ESOP. Companies with this type of cash and investments on hand, however, are rare.

Much has been written about the use of assets in existing retirement plans to partially fund a leveraged ESOP to reduce the amount of debt required to complete a transaction. Often, in closely held businesses the shareholders themselves function as trustees of 401(k) and profit-sharing plans. The idea of converting a portion of those assets into "equity" in a leveraged ESOP is difficult from a fiduciary standpoint. Keep in mind that they are selling shareholder-trustees of these retirement plans; as fiduciaries, they are acquiescing to the use of funds that are currently invested in a wide variety of debt and equity instruments that will now be invested in employer securities. This creates not only a fiduciary concern but also perhaps an elimination of an employee benefit. There have been cases involving existing retirement plans where a portion of those plans' assets have been converted to an ESOP. Although no one has indicated what might soften fiduciary responsibility when a selling shareholder is a trustee, there may be a conflict of interest concern if a shareholder-trustee uses more than 10% to 20% of the retirement plan assets in a new leveraged ESOP.

Many business owners try to accomplish as much as possible in a first-phase transaction. A very viable alternative is to scale back the size of the initial transaction to ease cash flow concerns. This also allows the company to continue growing even if the thought of leverage scares the business owner. Another possibility is for the company to initiate an unleveraged ESOP in which contributions for purchasing any employer's securities can be made. This allows the company to begin setting aside monies for the actual stock purchase at a later date. Then, when the selling shareholder is ready, the stock can be purchased either on an unleveraged basis, or on a leveraged basis that uses less debt than would be necessary on an unleveraged basis.

Conclusion

Leveraged ESOPs are viable alternatives as exit strategies. This form of recapitalization has excellent tax advantages not only for selling shareholders, but also for the company sponsoring the plan. The ability to pay back loans with pretax dollars is a tremendous advantage in any type of leveraged buyout. It is important, however, that a financial advisor structure the transaction so it does not encumber the business in a way that inhibits future growth. Structured properly and with great care to allow for amortizing the loan satisfactorily, the leveraged ESOP is a powerful tool in managing the transition of a business to the next generation, thus providing effective business succession planning.

Chapter 5

Senior Credit Underwriting for ESOP Transactions

Mary Sullivan Josephs

This chapter provides guidelines for companies, service providers, and lenders to better understand the unique characteristics of employee stock ownership plan (ESOP) transactions and how they are different from other term loans; basic underwriting guidelines, i.e., what lenders should consider in light of these differences; typical terms and conditions for an ESOP term loan; the role of Section 1042 replacement securities in credit structure; calculating cash flow available for debt service in S corporation and C corporation models; how to overcome common underwriting obstacles; and unique applications for ESOPs. By creatively structuring leveraged ESOPs with sound underwriting and attention to sellers' objectives, lenders will enjoy increased success in meeting the financing needs of both existing and prospective ESOP companies.

Unique Characteristics of ESOPs

On one hand, leveraged ESOPs do not differ significantly from other applications for term debt: the lender needs to evaluate the borrower's debt capacity for supporting the proposed credit. However, the unique characteristics of ESOPs, such as those detailed below, contribute to common underwriting confusion.

Nonproductive Debt

A leveraged ESOP often puts debt on the company's balance sheet without a corresponding increase in assets. Typical term loans finance growth or asset acquisitions through which the company projects to increase cash flow with an acceptable return on investment. Lenders need to (1) assess the total debt capacity of the company by deciding how much the company can borrow; (2) project and account for all forms of "productive" debt, including general working capital and term loans; and (3) calculate "debt capacity available for ESOP debt," the net result of (1) and (2) above. (Leveraged ESOPs also can be used as a financing vehicle for "productive" debt, involving an asset purchase or the refinance of existing debt. See "Basic Underwriting Guidelines" below for further explanation.)

Accounting Treatment

The stock bought in a leveraged ESOP is held, like treasury stock, in a contra-equity account until it is allocated to participants' accounts as the loan is paid off. This can create a negative tangible net worth and solvency issues. For example, in table 5-1, the company's equity declines from $6 million to negative $1 million as a result of accounting for the ESOP transaction.

TABLE 5-1. *Negative Net Worth Example.*

	Pre-ESOP	ESOP	Post-ESOP
Assets	$10,000,000	$ 0	$10,000,000
Liabilities	(4,000,000)	(7,000,000)	(11,000,000)
Equity	$ 6,000,000	$(7,000,000)	$ (1,000,000)
Leverage	.67x	N/A	$11,000,000 ÷ $ (1,000,000)

Employee Benefit Expense

With leveraged ESOPs, to the extent the company is allocating shares to participants' accounts (subject to Internal Revenue Code ["Code"] Section 415 and other restrictions that cap the maximum amount of employee benefits a company is able to expense), the repayment of debt can be "expensed." Debt can be repaid "above the line" instead of with after-tax cash flow. This "tax shield" related to ESOP debt makes ESOP debt significantly less expensive than other forms of debt (table 5-2).

In this example, the repayment of a similar $1 million loan payment saves the company $400,000 in taxes when paid as an ESOP

TABLE 5-2. *ESOP Tax Savings Example.*

	Non-ESOP Loan	ESOP Loan
Operating profit	$2,000,000	$2,000,000
ESOP payment	(0)	(1,000,000)
Pretax income	$2,000,000	$1,000,000
Taxes (40%)	(800,000)	(400,000)
Net profit	$1,200,000	$ 600,000
Loan payment	(1,000,000)	N/A
Net cash	$ 200,000	$ 600,000

loan versus a non-ESOP loan. If there were a $10,000,000 loan, the total tax shield over the term of the loan would be $4,000,000 ($400,000 tax shield per $1,000,000 × $10,000,000).

Employee Benefit Plan

An ESOP is an employee benefit plan. As such, it is subject to the Employee Retirement Income Security Act of 1974 (ERISA) and to scrutiny by the U.S. Department of Labor and the Internal Revenue Service. As such, there are fiduciary, administration, valuation, and human resources issues (among others) that must be taken into account in structuring the transaction. In non-ESOP transactions, a lender normally does not need to be sensitive to or even aware of such nonfinancial issues that are not directly related to the earnings-generating capacity of the company. Advising the company to engage an attorney specializing in ESOPs as well as a plan administrator is worthwhile, even in the design and feasibility stages of the transaction.

Section 1042 Benefit

Under Code Section 1042, when shares of a C corporation are sold to an ESOT (employee stock ownership trust) that owns 30% or more of the company, the seller can defer the capital gains tax obligation on proceeds from that sale so long as the seller reinvests proceeds in "qualified replacement property." It is advisable to consult a professional specializing in Section 1042 investment requirements to ensure proper investment of sales proceeds. In general, "qualified replacement property" includes stocks and bonds of domestic corporations. This advantageous tax treatment of Section 1042 for the selling shareholder is an important incentive for a seller to consider selling to the employees. Section 1042 also provides an asset that is very attractive collateral to lenders: cash. Section 1042 securities can be considered the "asset of last resort" in terms of a seller's willingness to pledge. While it may be discouraging to some sellers to pledge Section 1042 securities, it is important to recognize the benefits to the seller of selling to an ESOP, including among other things:

1. Gaining liquidity, and with less financial burden on the company than non-ESOP debt
2. Diversification of assets
3. Deferral of capital gains
4. Opportunity for estate planning
5. Ownership transition
6. Increased flexibility in work schedule if desired
7. Continued involvement if desired
8. Creating employee ownership

Pledging some or all of the Section 1042 proceeds may be a reasonable price to pay in the short run in order to achieve the seller's long-term objectives. For example, table 5-3 assumes a $10 million sale regardless if the sale is to a third party or an ESOP. There is a $2 million cash advantage to the seller if the ESOP is chosen as the sales vehicle.

TABLE 5-3. *Seller's Section 1042 Benefit.*

	Non-ESOP	ESOP
Sales proceeds	$10,000,000	$10,000,000
Capital gains tax (20%)	(2,000,000)	N/A
Net proceeds to seller	$ 8,000,000	$10,000,000

Trends in ESOP Transactions

S Corporation ESOPs

Notwithstanding the compelling benefits of Section 1042, an increasing number of S corporation owners are choosing to forego the Section 1042 election, pay capital gains, and have their companies retain S corporation status. Section 1042 is available only if the ESOP company is a C corporation at the time of the transaction. If a company is a C corporation before the transaction, the strategy is often to get to 100% ESOP ownership as quickly as possible, thus maximizing the tax benefits under Section 1042, and then to elect S status and enjoy the tax benefits of being exempt from federal income taxes. Companies that are S corporations before the transaction (and this is very common among middle-market companies because of the single taxation to S corporation shareholders and the extremely favorable tax treatment advantages S corporations have upon the sale of the business), on the other hand, can often maximize their tax benefits by retaining their S corporation status. This is an excellent strategy in partial liquidity scenarios where the shareholders are not certain of their ultimate exit strategy. The S corporation has some attractive tax considerations upon the ultimate sale of the business that are more difficult to obtain as a C corporation. Though merger and acquisition tax issues are not discussed in this chapter, it is important to point out their role in the growing trend of business owners to not elect the Section 1042 tax deferral. Benefits of not electing Section 1042 treatment include the ability to retain S status and protect the favorable tax treatment of an ultimate asset sale. Upon a non-ESOP sale of an S corporation meeting certain requirements, if such sale is an asset sale, the S-corporation shareholder merely pays capital gains on the sale of assets, not ordinary income. In contrast, with a non-ESOP asset sale in a C corporation, the company needs to pay corporate-level taxes on the sale of assets, and then the shareholder needs to pay (under current tax law) an incremental 15% dividend tax. This adds up to approximately a 55% tax for an asset sale in a C corporation environment versus a 15% tax for an ultimate asset sale in an S corporation environment.

Another benefit of retaining S status in partial liquidity scenarios is that the selling shareholders and their family members can participate in the ESOP. This ability to participate in the ESOP often mitigates having to pay capital gains on the proceeds of the sale to the ESOP. A further S corporation structuring issue that lenders should bear in mind is the accumulated adjustments account, which represents the accumulation of already taxed profits in an S corporation. A shareholder can withdraw tax-free from the accumulated adjustments account at any time. It is often the first liquidity step an S corporation shareholder takes.

Larger Deals

Another current trend is larger deals. Valuation issues aside, the two contributing factors are C corporation "options" and the desire to be a 100% S corporation ESOP. There is some challenge from certain offices of the IRS as to whether or not an "option" is a valid security to be held by an ESOP. Until this came up for debate, it was not unusual, for example, for a seller to sell 30% to the ESOT to be eligible for deferral of capital gains and also give the ESOT an option to purchase the next 21% so as to avoid the minority interest discount that would otherwise be ascribed to a minority interest transaction. Another force behind larger ESOP transactions is the phenomenon of companies attempting to become 100% ESOP-owned S corporations in order to be completely exempt from federal income taxes. Larger deals often lead to larger gaps (see the discussion of collateral shortfall later in this chapter). One solution to the "gap" is seller notes. The problem with seller notes is that if the seller does not receive the physical proceeds, he or she cannot actually invest in qualified replacement property (unless the seller has sufficient other funds to do so). The financial markets have developed a strategy such that the seller can borrower against the proceeds they do receive in order to create a larger portfolio, effectively shielding the full value for purposes of deferral of capital gains.

In order to evidence the proceeds physically going in and out of the ESOP for the monetization strategy mentioned above, lenders are often asked to make a "day loan." The day loan is issued and repaid on the day of closing and is of minimal risk to the lending institution (see figure 5-1).

Basic Underwriting Guidelines

The specific credit considerations for ESOP transactions are not materially different from normal term loan underwriting. With that being said, the weighting the underwriter gives to various credit underwriting considerations does differ with ESOPs.

Management

Although management is an important factor in every credit situation, the issue is even more pertinent with ESOPs. If the founder is

Figure 5-1. Day Loan Schematic

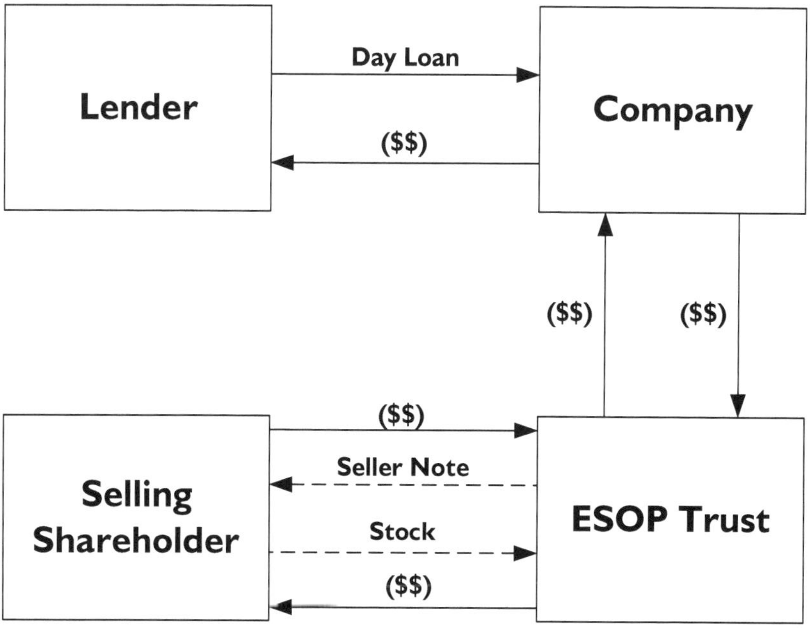

selling out or just backing out, the lender will need to be confident that the replacement management team can continue to generate the earnings level that the lender is underwriting.

Purpose

The lender must understand all the varying objectives of a particular transaction. The transaction structure can differ depending on the underlying objectives. Examples of different applications for a leveraged ESOPs include:

- *Nonproductive Debt:*
  1. To achieve full or partial liquidity for a closely held business owner through the owner selling existing shares to the ESOP (figure 5-2).
  2. Second-stage ESOP transactions.
  3. To attain liquidity on a tax-advantaged basis, using Section 1042 securities for deferral of capital gains on the securities (but not all transactions are motivated by Section 1042).
  4. To facilitate a MBO (management buyout).
  5. Public-to-private transactions.
  6. Corporate spinoffs.
  7. To achieve full or partial liquidity for a closely held business owner through the company issuing new shares of stock, selling those shares to the ESOP, and using the cash proceeds to provide liquidity to the owner (figure 5-3).

- *Productive Debt:*
  1. To refinance existing debt on a tax-advantaged basis with debt repayments "above the line" (see "Employee Benefit Expense" above).
  2. To issue new debt on a tax-advantaged basis with debt repayments "above the line."
  3. Making an acquisition.

Figure 5-2. Leveraged ESOP Transaction in Which ESOP Purchases Existing Shares

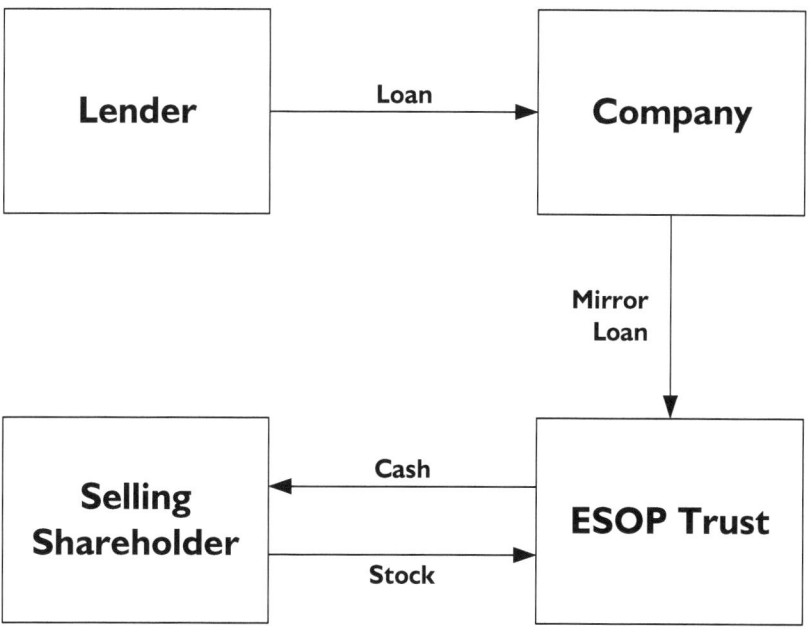

Figure 5-3. Leveraged ESOP Transaction in Which ESOP Purchases Newly Issued Shares

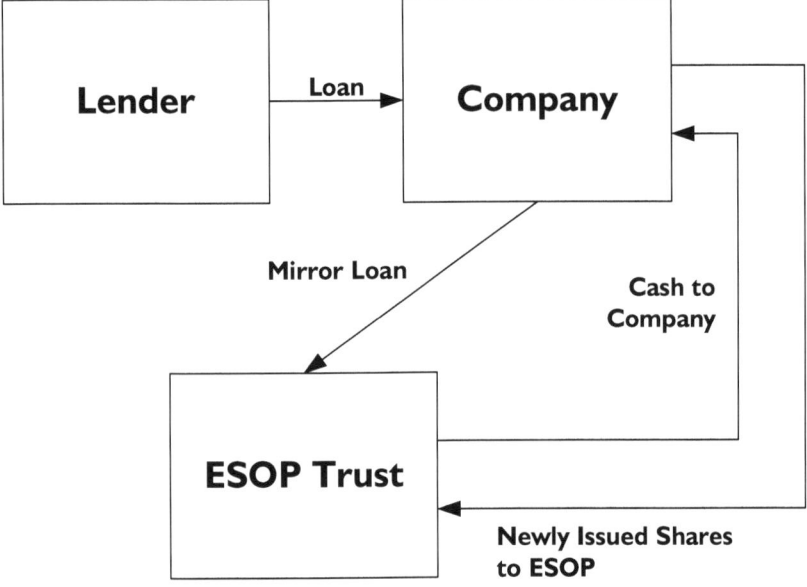

Depending on the purpose of the leveraged ESOP, the debt can be considered "productive" or "nonproductive." Generally, productive debt adds debt to a balance sheet with a corresponding asset addition. The incremental debt is used to purchase an asset or assets that produce incremental cash flow for the company. Ideally, the cash flow generated from the asset purchase is more than sufficient to service the incremental debt. In addition to the incremental cash flow, the asset itself will have collateral loan value to the lender. The incremental cash flow and loan value of the asset both enhance the proposed senior credit underwriting.

With nonproductive debt, a liability is added to the balance sheet without a corresponding addition of income-producing hard assets. "Soft" issues such as a projected increase in margins attributable to employee ownership are difficult for a lender to underwrite. On the other hand, add-backs of nonrecurring historical expenses such as the owner's salary and historical employee benefit expenses are considered in the underwriting process. Ideally, the debt is serviced with the existing asset base and existing cash flow plus "add-backs" (see "Cash Flow Available for Debt Service" below for further explanation of add-backs).

As depicted in figure 5-3, new shares of stock can be issued to facilitate tax-advantaged financing. Both the existing shareholders and the company need to take into account the impact of dilution on share value when using this strategy. For example, if a company has an enterprise value of $20 million and 200 shares of stock outstanding, the value per share is $100,000. If this company were to issue 50 new shares of stock, each share would then be worth only $80,000 ($20 million ÷ 250 shares). The 50 new shares are worth $4 million (50 shares × $80,000 per share). However, the pre-existing 200 shares are only worth $16 million (200 shares × $80,000 per share). Presuming the company was using this $4 million to refinance existing non-ESOP debt, there could be a $1,600,000 tax shield ($4 million × 40% tax rate) created to partially offset the negative impact of dilution.

Cash Flow Available for Debt Service

Cash flow available for debt service is a critical underwriting concept for all credit. The lender needs to feel comfortable the company has sufficient cash flow to service the proposed credit request. A common benchmark to determine debt service is EBITDA (earnings before interest, taxes, depreciation, and amortization). Lenders must consider what other claims exist on cash flow in addition to debt service. Examples include required maintenance and capital expenditures, lease payments, and other fixed charges. With a retailer, for example, the company has considerable capital expenditures each year to keep the stores updated. If the company does not make certain capital expenditures, its business will suffer.

Therefore, a more prudent calculation of cash flow available for debt service is EBITDA less (1) required capital expenditures for ongoing operations, (2) required cash flow to service other non-ESOP debt, and (3) other necessary claims on cash flow for a particular company and industry. With ESOPs, to determine cash flow available for debt service, simply add "add-backs" to the result of the above. Common add-backs of nonrecurring historical expenses include:

- Salary and other compensation attributable to a departing shareholder.
- Compensation reductions contemplated as a result of the transaction.
- Other expenses related to the owner that the company will not cover going forward.
- Historical 401(k) matching and profit sharing expenses to the extent the previous employee benefit will be replaced by the ESOP benefit.
- Historical losses from nonrecurring events.

The example in table 5-4 demonstrates the significance of the above variables in determining cash flow available for ESOP debt service. The preexisting requirements for cash flow such as required capital expenditures and existing debt service cannot be ignored. However, add-backs and other adjustments from nonrecurring expenses can offset their impact on cash flow available for debt service.

TABLE 5-4. *Cash Flow Available for Debt Service.*

EBITDA	$2,000,000
Less: required capital expenditures	(500,000)
P&I for existing debt	(500,000)
EBITDA available for new debt service	$1,000,000
Plus: departing owner's salary	600,000
Historical employee benefit expense	200,000
Nonrecurring legal expenses	250,000
EBITDAE available for ESOP debt	$2,050,000

Modeling the Tax Shield to Assess Net Cash Flow Available for Debt Service and Fixed Charge Coverage Ratios

C Corporations

For a C corporation, the maximum tax shield for the ESOP debt (non-ESOP debt has no tax shield) is 25% of covered payroll. A company may exceed this limitation by issuing a "reasonable" dividend (typically 10%–15% of value) "above the line." However,

1. The maximum allowable dividend cannot exceed the "reasonable" standard. Therefore, in many cases it is impossible to truly drive taxes to zero.

2. The company must allocate a comparable amount of stock to the participants' accounts. By overaccelerating the stock contribution, the company could be inadvertently creating a human resource issue for newer employees who will not have the opportunity to participate as much as they had intended.

3. The dividend is a preference item for purposes of calculating the alternative minimum tax (AMT). Thus, a company still may not achieve a reduced tax rate.

4. The dividend could be paid on all shares. Unless the ESOP is a separate class of stock (acceptable only for C corporations) or owns 100% of the company, cash intended for debt service could inadvertently flow to non-ESOP shareholders.

Precision is imperative in calculating the true tax shield in order to avoid overstating projected cash flow in the underwriting.

S Corporations

For an S corporation, allocations must be made using the principal-and-interest method, thus exhausting the 25% cap more quickly. Once again, it is important to avoid inadvertently overstating cash flow available for debt service by misrepresenting the tax shield. Implications are different for 100% ESOP-owned S corporations and partially ESOP-owned S corporations.

For a partially ESOP-owned S corporation, the non-ESOP shareholder will be required to pay taxes on its percentage of income earned. Typically, an S corporation dividends (in S corporation terms, "distributes") to the owner the amount needed to pay taxes. Because there can be only one class of stock in an S corporation, the same cash dividend must also go to the ESOP. Because the ESOP does not have a tax obligation, the ESOP can either (1) keep the cash in the plan to fund future acquisitions or for repurchase obligation protection, or (2) dividend (prepay the internal loan) the cash back to the company.

Only the portion of cash attributable to *unallocated* shares may be dividended back to the company for potential debt service. Clearly, this is not an issue in the first year of the transaction when all shares are unallocated. In subsequent years, as the ESOP shares are released into plan participant accounts via "employee benefit expense" or as the internal ESOP loan is repaid from the dividend back to the company commensurate with the percent of unallocated shares, a smaller portion of the cash that the ESOP earns from its share of the tax distribution can be given back to the company for corporate use. Prepaying the internal ESOP loan exacerbates the problem because it causes an accelerated release of shares into participants' accounts, increasing the ratio of allocated shares, reducing the cash that can go back to the company in future years. This may have significant debt service implications. Once again, it is imperative that the true tax shield be calculated correctly to ensure adequate debt service coverage.

Factoring the Repurchase Obligation into the Cash Flow Available for Debt Service

In closely held companies, ESOP shares have a mandatory put option such that vested participants who leave the company have the ability to put distributed shares back to the sponsor company in exchange for the current fair market value of the stock (based on an annual valuation of the ESOP shares). The company has the obligation to buy back those shares in a manner consistent with plan documents. (Note that distributions of leveraged shares generally may be deferred until the loan that bought those shares is repaid.) In first-time ESOP transactions that do not use a rollover of other plan assets as a source of equity, the shares have not generally been allocated and/or vested sufficiently to cause concern with any material accumulation of unforeseen expenses. The deferral of the put option (but for death, disability, and retirement) gives the lender further comfort that the repurchase obligation will not cause an unforeseen drain on cash flow.

In second-stage transactions, mature employee-owned companies, and transactions where a rollover of existing plan assets serves as a source of funds for the transaction, lenders need to project repurchase obligations into the cash flow analysis. Some companies develop their own models, as they truly have a good sense of retirement patterns. Larger companies use one of a few software products that have actuarially based models to aid in forecasting. The repurchase obligation, though not required by GAAP to be listed on the balance sheet, is a real pre-cash-flow, available-for-debt-service obligation of the company, and it must be considered in subsequent years of all ESOP transactions.

A lender cannot possibly have an accurate account of cash flow available for debt service without accurately modeling both the tax shield and the repurchase obligation.

How Covenants Work

Covenants are part of nearly every loan agreement. However, some of the lender's favorite covenants, minimum tangible net worth and maximum leverage (total liabilities to tangible net worth), lose their efficacy in light of the contra-equity accounting in leveraged ESOPs. Lenders need to focus instead on:

- Cash flow, as defined by minimum EBITDAE (earnings before interest, taxes, depreciation, amortization, and employee benefits expense). This benchmark is set to ensure the company meets minimum earning thresholds to service debt.

- The debt service coverage ratio, which is defined as the ratio of EBITDAE to all required principal and interest payments. The benchmark will vary depending on the deal structure. For example, fully secured credits may require 1:1 coverage whereas a "cash flow" structure may require 1:2 or greater coverage.
- Leverage, which is more effectively defined as senior debt to EBITDAE in ESOP transactions.
- Interest coverage (EBITDAE/interest expense) and fixed charge coverage (EBITDAE/fixed charges) ratios also are helpful in monitoring the financial leverage and debt service capability of the company.

Projected Financial Information

Lenders know that they are not experts in a particular company's business. Therefore, the lender needs to be comfortable that the company thoroughly understands the risks, opportunities, and market dynamics of its business niche. For leveraged ESOP term loans, most lenders will require five years of detailed pro-forma financial statements from the company. The lender uses this primarily to calculate debt service coverage for the proposed transaction. It is critical in ESOP underwriting to assess the quality of historical earnings and use that as a benchmark to project future earnings. A lender needs to work closely with the CFO and/or financial advisor to the company to reconcile historical numbers, identify and reconcile add-backs, and develop projections and sensitivity analysis. Lenders are not looking for "hockey stick" projections where revenues and margins are going to explode because a new widget is brought to market. A rational best-case scenario, using well-founded assumptions, goes much further toward proving to the lender a company's thorough understanding of its marketplace.

Working with Experienced Service Providers

With ESOP transactions, it is important to have confidence in each of the parties to the transaction. The lender is underwriting its customer, the company. However, with ESOPs, a lender should also evaluate the financial advisor, trustee, plan administrator, and legal counsel. Though it would be unusual for the senior lender to be liable in the event of plan disqualification, plan disqualification does have significant cash flow implications that could affect a company's ability to meet the proposed debt service requirements. For example, if a plan with a $10 million loan were disqualified, the loan would have to be repaid with after-tax dollars, much like any other non-ESOP corporate debt. This would increase the cash flow required to service the debt by approximately $4 million, assuming a 40% corporate tax rate.

Financial Reporting

Because of the leveraging impact of the ESOP, to the extent the lender is relying on the corporate (not personal) assets and cash flow, it is likely the company will be required to have audited financial statements annually. Monthly reporting may include a borrowing base certificate detailing current assets and revolver activity (see "Borrowing Base Certificate" below). This differs from non-ESOP middle-market transactions, in which deals can get done on reviewed or compiled numbers.

Collateral Analysis

The package of corporate assets is unchanged in ESOPs as compared to non-ESOPs. However, because of the leveraging impact of the "nonproductive" ESOP debt when the ESOP is used to buy out an owner, the lender has greater reliance on these assets. Typical, "rule of thumb" advance rates on corporate assets are:

- *Eligible Accounts Receivable: 80%.* If the company sells solely to top-credit quality customers with nominal bad debt experience, a higher advance rate may be warranted. Similarly, if the company has significant account dilution and/or write-offs, the advance rate on accounts receivable may be less than 80%. Eligibility criteria typically excludes from the borrowing base inter-company and related party receivables, foreign receivables, receivables over 90 days past due, and so on.
- *Eligible Inventory: 50%.* If raw materials or finished goods inventory consist of a commodity, such as paper, steel, cocoa beans, and so on, higher advance rates may be warranted. High per-

ishability and obsolescence or lack of marketability may negatively affect the advance rates. Work in process is almost always considered ineligible. Eligibility of finished goods varies from company to company. To the extent finished goods are highly proprietary to a particular customer, with limited alternative applications, advance rates will be low to nothing. Lastly, in asset-based transactions, the lender may cap inventory borrowings regardless of what the borrowing base may suggest.

- *Real Estate: 0% to 70%.* First, the lender and company will have to resolve all environmental issues, regardless of whether the lender is actually taking a mortgage on the property. The market value will be ascertained from a third-party appraiser hired by the lender. The loan value of the real estate is usually 70% of the market value less 100% of any existing liens and encumbrances. It is unusual to have a more aggressive advance than 70%. Factors that would influence a smaller advance include limited alternative uses for the facility, poor geographic location of the facility, and perceived environmental risks of the facility.

- *Fixed Assets: 50% of book value.* 50% of book value is a good rule of thumb. However, if a lender is truly relying on the fixed assets of a particular company, an independent appraisal from a third party is solicited. Advance rates on the appraised value are typically 75% of orderly liquidation value or 90% of "under the hammer" or "fire sale" liquidation. The fixed asset appraisal will, as with the real estate appraisal, need to be performed by an independent third party hired by the lender.

Borrowing Base Certificate

The exact form of a borrowing base certificate will vary from lender to lender. The concept, nonetheless, is similar—to evidence at regular intervals (anywhere from daily to monthly depending on the loan structure) the loan value of the assets. The lender then compares the loan value of the assets with the credit outstanding at that same time. The borrowing base certificate is the means by which the lender limits total credit outstanding and ensures the borrower cannot borrow in excess of the proposed collateral structure. A borrower is "capped," unable to borrow in excess of the limits of its borrowing base certificate. In table 5-5, even though the borrower has a $12

TABLE 5-5. Basic Borrowing Base Certificate for Current Assets.

Asset	Gross Value	Advance Rate	Loan Value
Accounts receivable	$10,000,000	80%	$ 8,000,000
Inventory	$ 5,000,000	50%	2,500,000
Eligible borrowing base			$10,500,000
Less: revolving line of credit outstanding			(10,000,000)
Amount available to be drawn under the $12,000,000 line of credit			$ 500,000

million revolving line of credit, its borrowing base certificate restricts its total borrowings to $10.5 million. Because, in this example, the borrower already has $10 million outstanding under the line, it can borrow only an additional $500,000 at this point.

Collateral Shortfall

The ESOP credit request often results in a collateral shortfall. The loan value of the assets is insufficient to cover the basic borrowing needs of the company and the ESOP debt.

As table 5-6 illustrates, the ESOP debt request can create a shortfall in asset coverage. Resolving this shortfall issue is the part of the "art" of structuring the ESOP transaction. (See "Overcoming Common Underwriting Obstacles" below for a discussion of how to cover a collateral shortfall.)

Typical Terms and Conditions for ESOP Term Loans

Borrower

ESOP loans are preferably made directly to the company, not to the ESOT itself. This way, the lender makes a loan directly to the ultimate source of repayment. It is possible to loan to the ESOT with a guarantee from the company. This is certainly considered in situations where there are structuring obstacles to lending directly to the company (for example, where push-down accounting is to be

TABLE 5-6. Example of an ESOP Term Loan Creating a Collateral Shortfall.

Asset	Gross Value	Advance Rate	Loan Value
Accounts receivable	$10,000,000	80%	$ 8,000,000
Inventory	$ 5,000,000	50%	2,500,000
Real estate	$ 5,000,000	70%	3,500,000
Fixed assets	$ 8,000,000	50%	4,000,000
Total loan value of collateral			$ 18,000,000
Less: existing revolver and term debt requirements			(10,000,000)
Collateral available for ESOP term loan			$ 8,000,000
Less: ESOP term loan			(20,000,000)
Collateral shortfall			$(12,000,000)

avoided, where the loan is secured by Section 1042 assets, or where there are regulatory issues). Figure 5-2 above shows the funds flow for a loan directly to the company. Figure 5-4 details the funds flow for a loan to the ESOP trust with a collateralized guarantee from the company.

Credit Facilities

Generally, lenders will structure the revolving line of credit as a separate credit facility from term debt. Theoretically, the revolving line of credit should be secured by the current assets of the company supporting the short-term working capital borrowings. The term debt is then secured by the fixed (long-term) assets of a company. Real estate loans are often structured as separate loans as well. With an ESOP loan, there are usually at least two credit facilities, a working capital revolving credit facility, and an ESOP term loan. There could be a third or fourth facility for real estate or other term debt. Sometimes lenders structure the undersecured or cash flow portion of the term loan as a separate credit facility with a different interest rate and amortization structure than the fully secured facilities.

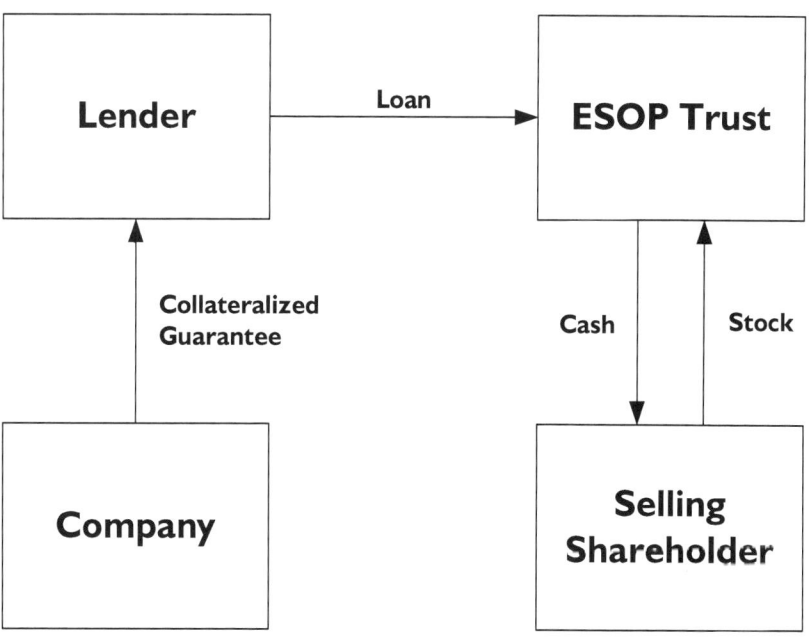

Figure 5-4. Leveraged ESOP Transaction in Which the Loan Is Made Directly to the ESOP Trust

Facility A: Working Capital Revolving Credit Facility

It is imperative that the lender consider all borrowing needs of the company in conjunction with the ESOP. A lender generally prefers to have long-term debt secured by the long-term assets and current debt secured by the current assets. With a strong company that has historically self-financed its working capital needs, there can be an "overcollateralized" position with respect to current assets covering revolver needs and an "undercollateralized" position with respect to long-term assets covering term debt needs. In this situation, some lenders will find it acceptable to secure all or part of the ESOP term debt with current assets. This can be done formally with a "block" on the borrowing base as illustrated by table 5-7, or informally with a minimum availability covenant. With the BBC (borrowing base certificate) in table 5-7, a "block" would be executed for a company with a $13 million current asset loan value and revolver needs that are never projected to exceed $9 million.

In this example, the first $4 million of availability would always be used to support the term loans outstanding, reducing the revolver availability.

TABLE 5-7. Borrowing Base Certificate Using Short-Term Assets to "Cover" Collateral Needs for Term Loan.

	Eligible Asset Value	Advance Rate	Loan Value of Asset
Accounts receivable	$10,000,000	80%	$ 8,000,000
Inventory	$10,000,000	50%	5,000,000
Total available for borrowing			$13,000,000
Less: "block" for term loan collateral			(4,000,000)
Total available for revolver borrowing			$ 9,000,000

Facility B: ESOP Term Loan

Current market conditions price term debt similar to revolving debt, particularly when they are both multi-year facilities, cross-collateralized and cross-defaulted.

Amortization

The amortization period is typically five to seven years, depending on structure and debt service ability. Fully secured loans can sustain a longer amortization schedule than cash flow loans. Cash flow loans are required to be amortized over five years to seven years. Since Code Section 133 (which provided a tax incentive for ESOP lenders) was repealed in 1996, lenders have no longer been concerned about exact mirror loan provisions under which the principal repayments on ESOP loans mirror the benefit allocation. Therefore, a borrower can, with after-tax cash flow, repay the bank debt faster than the actual benefits are allocated.

Rate

The rate varies depending on leverage and debt service coverage. LIBOR (London Inter-Bank Offer Rate) is a common pricing benchmark as an alternative to prime. It is common for lenders to propose a pricing grid that commits to price reductions as the leverage decreases due to either debt repayment and/or earnings increases (table 5-8).

TABLE 5-8. *Example Performance Pricing Matrix.*

Cash Flow Leverage Ratio	Loan Pricing Spread over LIBOR
Greater than 3.25:1	300
Between 3.00 and 3.25:1	250
Between 2.50 and 3.00:1	225
Between 2.00 and 2.50:1	200
Less than 2.00:1	175

Closing Fee

Commitment fees range from .5% to 3.0% on ESOP accommodations. Factors that warrant the higher end of the fee range include highly leveraged transactions; highly complex transactions; syndicated and/or underwritten transactions where the lender assumes the syndication risk; and cash flow-based, substantially undersecured transactions. Factors that warrant the lower end of the fee range include lower leverage, ample collateral, and highly competitive situations.

Non-use Fee

A facility fee ranging from 1/8% to .75% is charged on the unused portion of line commitments. This fee compensates the lender for reserves (direct costs to the lender) that must be held on commitments upon which there are no borrowings (revenues to lender to offset costs). One strategy to reduce non-use fees is to structure the line with seasonal increases as needed, minimizing the unused commitment.

Collateral

A blanket lien on all corporate assets is fairly standard. If the transaction is an unsecured transaction, it is not unusual for lenders to require a "negative pledge" and/or a "springing lien." With a negative pledge, a company agrees not to pledge unencumbered assets to another party during the term of the loan. A springing lien sets forth parameters that would give the lender the right to encumber the unencumbered assets of the company.

Guarantees

Guarantees are definitely not part of every ESOP loan. Credit enhancement for undersecured credits can come in a variety of forms. A popular method to fill the gap is use of Section 1042 proceeds as collateral via a pledge or collateralized guarantee from the seller (see the Section 1042 discussion below). Sometimes the full or partial guarantee may be satisfactory without the collateral pledge. The existence and structure of a guarantee varies greatly from transaction to transaction.

Conditions Precedent

Because of the complexities of the ESOP, certain other conditions are likely to be required that are not part of a non-ESOP loan. For example:

- *Acceptable valuation firm:* The lender will want to ensure that the "adequate consideration" opinion is provided by an independent, experienced, and reputable firm.

- *Acceptable trustee:* Many transactions employ outside fiduciaries to represent the buyer, the ESOT. The lender will want to verify the independence and prudence of whoever is serving as the trustee.
- *Acceptable and independent counsel representing the ESOT:* It is advisable that experienced ESOP counsel represent the trustee to minimize future complications, not the least of which could potentially be plan disqualification and/or fiduciary impropriety.
- *Satisfactory repurchase obligation study:* Pre-transaction repurchase obligation studies are not usually necessary in first-stage transactions. Nonetheless, it is advisable for the lender to encourage the company to begin thinking about and planning for the repurchase obligation.

Solvency

In a leveraged ESOP transaction, stock purchased by the ESOP is held as treasury stock until released gradually into plan participants' accounts, often resulting in negative total net worth. Notwithstanding other issues effecting solvency, this "accounting" issue is typically addressed through the signing of a "solvency affidavit." With this affidavit, counsel has advised that the bank is protected from fraudulent conveyance issues. In highly structured multi-investor transactions, bank lenders have asked to receive a solvency opinion or to be permitted to rely on the solvency opinion rendered to the trustee.

Solvency Opinion

In multi-investor transactions, trustees increasingly ask for a solvency opinion from an independent valuation firm. Lenders should ask to be included in the solvency opinion whenever it is a trustee's requirement.

Legal Documents

Loan documents, from the lender's perspective, do not differ materially for an ESOP loan versus a similar non-ESOP term loan. It may seem more onerous, particularly if the company has not historically borrowed on a secured or highly leveraged basis. Notwithstanding the ESOP loan's similarity to other term loans, the lender should choose attorneys who are very experienced with ESOPs. It is important for the lender to feel comfortable with the integrity of the overall transaction.

The Role of Section 1042 Proceeds in Credit Structure

Having the 1042 replacement securities serve as collateral is by no means a given in every ESOP transaction. However, in the event that Section 1042 is the full or partial solution to a collateral shortfall (see table 5-6 above for an example of a $12 million shortfall), the following issues should be considered.

Advance Rate on 1042 Assets

Advance rates for marketable securities vary depending on the perceived riskiness of the security. Table 5-9 gives typical margin guidelines for lenders. Lenders require an advance rate, or "margin" to provide a cushion for both marketability of the security and the inevitable valuation fluctuations.

TABLE 5-9. *Margin Requirements for Lenders: Advance Rates for Marketable Securities.*

Marketable Security Pledged	Advance Rate on Security
Listed stock	70%
Corporate bonds: maturity of five years or less	85%
Corporate bonds: maturity of more than five years	80%

If a lender were to strictly adhere to the advance rates in table 5-9, a seller would actually need to post collateral plus the margin "cushion." For example, if the seller invested rollover proceeds in a New York Stock Exchange stock portfolio, technically, in order for the seller to completely cover a $12 million collateral shortfall on a fully margined basis, the seller would need to pledge $17.1 million ($12 million divided by .7) in collateral.

Release Provisions for 1042 Assets

Release provisions for Section 1042 assets (i.e., the seller's qualified replacement property) held as collateral can be important to the seller. On the most conservative side, Section 1042 assets would be pledged on a fully margined basis up front and then released pro rata as the loan is paid down. Other ideas include:

- Structuring the ESOP loan to not require Section 1042 qualified replacement property to be in margin initially, and commencing the release of Section 1042 qualified replacement property from collateral once the loan is in margin and the loan value of the collateral (securities times advance rate) equals the principal outstanding.
- Accelerating the release of qualified replacement property from collateral as leverage (the ratio of funded debt to EBITDAE) decreases. For example, a loan that may need to be fully secured when the leverage is 4:1 can release qualified replacement property from collateral when leverage falls below 2:1.
- Releasing qualified replacement property from collateral if the company achieves certain minimum EBITDAE levels. This strategy is particularly helpful in a transaction where cash flow projections are significantly improved from historical cash flows. In a sense, the seller "underwrites" the promised improvements. When the improvements are realized, the collateral is released.
- "Sharing" of the release. In situations where the initial credit structure includes a partial pledge of Section 1042 assets and a portion of unsecured credit exposure, the lender may want to be in a fully margined position before the release of the seller's pledge. This could conflict with the seller's objectives to accelerate the release of his or her collateral pledge. A compromise structure allows a partial release of qualified replacement property from collateral for each dollar of principal reduction. For example, for every dollar of principal reduction, the lender could release 50 cents of securities held as collateral.
- The seller often successfully negotiates the retention of interest earned on the qualified replacement property so long as the principal amount of the securities stays within the required margin.

- Distribution of asset appreciation is also a point of negotiation. As long as there are no defaults in the loan agreement and no financial deterioration in the portfolio held as collateral, the seller can negotiate to have any appreciation in the account swept out of the "collateral" account and into an unpledged account on a regular basis.

Covenants and Section 1042 Collateral

There are additional covenant considerations in loans where marketable securities are held as collateral. Most notably, a trigger for minimum market value of the marketable securities portfolio may be used. For example, a covenant may specify that if the portfolio falls below 80% of the required market value of the collateral, it will trigger a default in the loan agreement.

Overcoming Common Underwriting Obstacles

The nonproductive debt, the negative tangible net worth, the complexity of ESOP financing as it interrelates with so many other disciplines, the fiduciary risk, and the typical desire by sellers to limit their personal pledge of Section 1042 assets all serve to heighten the complexity of ESOP financing. A financing transaction that on one hand could be looked at like any other credit request becomes fairly complex when an ESOP is involved. Knowledge of how to creatively overcome the underwriting obstacles, as described below, can help sellers, companies, and service providers in choosing the best lender for their particular transaction and can help lenders successfully underwrite these transactions.

What Is an ESOP? Educating the Lender

Lenders need to be educated on the peculiarities of an ESOP transaction, including the accounting treatment, the difference between the inside and outside loan, fiduciary issues, benefit administration, and allocation issues. A lender needs to understand that benefit restrictions can limit the amount a company can "expense" in a given year. Loans need to be thoughtfully and prudently structured around such limitations. The ESOP could, for example, impair a company's ability to meet a standard cash flow recapture provision.

Although it is advisable to work with an experienced ESOP lender whenever possible, working with an existing financial institution may provide a company greater comfort, debt capacity, and financial flexibility. This is due to such an institution's competitive advantage in understanding a particular company's business. Introduce your lender to experienced financial advisors, attorneys, and plan administrators early in the feasibility process to give the lender sufficient time to learn and understand the nuances of the ESOP transaction.

Historical Financial Information

Often, an ESOP prospect has not previously borrowed much beyond a typical working capital line of credit with its local lender. Typically, the company has not been required to provide audited financials. The quality of reported earnings has never been questioned. The company has typically never been subject to the extensive due diligence on the historical financials that will be part of leveraged ESOP underwriting. Companies may resist, finding the process overwhelming and intrusive.

Overcoming this problem: The purpose of the lender's due diligence is to gain comfort with the company's historical ability to generate cash flow and use that as a benchmark to predict the company's future ability to do so. It is critical to the lender that the company assist in this process. It is an opportunity for the company to begin to partner with the lender. The better the lender understands the historical financial information and the company's revenue and margin sensitivities, the more confident the lender will be in calculating senior debt capacity for the borrower. Greater senior debt capacity has several advantages to the seller and company, such as favorable pricing, less of a pledge of Section 1042 assets in Section 1042 deals, less need for mezzanine and equity investors, and avoiding the complexities of multi-investor transactions.

Alternatives for evaluating historical numbers: In some instances, the lender will require an independent auditor to audit historical numbers. This is costly in both money and time. Alternatives include: (1) an audit of only the income statement, (2) third-party due diligence, and (3) the bank sending out its own field auditors to examine the books and records of the company.

Out of Size, Out of Market

A company should always strive to be in an important relationship to its primary financial institution. This means being the right size for its lender. It is not advisable to be either the smallest or largest client relationship for a lender. Therefore, smaller transactions are often best served with local banks. Unfortunately, the technical sophistication required for ESOP lending is often not found in these smaller financial institutions, and the larger financial institutions are not interested in traveling to remote locations for smaller-sized transactions.

Overcoming this problem: If the hurdle to educating the lender is too large, or the proposed ESOP transaction causes a company to "outgrow" its existing financial institution, a new lender may be necessary. To source an experienced lender, a company should talk with local attorneys, financial advisors, and plan administrators who have worked on ESOP transactions, call local companies who have ESOPs in place, and use the resources of organizations such as the NCEO and the ESOP Association for leads.

Lack of Creativity

ESOPs can be nonproductive debt. Lenders need to think creatively and understand how the ESOP fits into the whole context of the corporate and shareholder's objectives. Because these objectives can vary so much, each ESOP tends to have a unique structure.

Overcoming lack of creativity: For straightforward transactions in a more generic industry that do not burden the company's debt capacity, financing may be available from local or existing lenders. For more creative structures, a company will need to be more aggressive in their search process. The NCEO and the ESOP Association are excellent resources for names of companies and/or professionals who have participated in recent or similar ESOP transactions. In highly complex transactions, engaging a financial advisor to assist in deal structure, lender education, and debt placement can also prove beneficial.

What Is an ESOP? Educating Your Controller/CFO

The complexities of putting a leveraged ESOP in place often exceed the experience of the company's controller or chief financial officer.

The lender will require significant forecasting and sensitivity analysis. The CFO will likely be responsible for negotiating the terms and conditions of the loan agreement without the requisite experience. However, the company typically does not have a long-term need for a CFO with higher credentials.

Overcoming this problem: Working with an experienced lender and an experienced financial advisor can mitigate this problem. Another solution is to formally engage a financial advisor to the transaction. This could be the company's accountant, an investment banker, an independent financial consultant, or a valuation professional. Financial advisors representing the company prepare the detailed forecasts and financial analysis that lenders require. To the extent the lender better understands the financial sensitivities of the company, the company may be able to negotiate more competitive credit arrangements. A company might also consider introducing its chief financial officer to CFOs from other ESOP companies to exchange ideas and information. Names of companies and candidates who may be interested in such networking are available through the NCEO and the ESOP Association.

What Is an ESOP? Educating the Lender's Loan Committee

Even when the loan officer understands ESOPs and ESOP lending, it won't help the company unless the financing institution's loan committee is also familiar with the particularities that make ESOP transactions look different from the typical deal they see. It is not unusual for an ESOP deal to get turned down or restructured in the loan committee process.

Overcoming this problem: Due diligence is not a one-way process solely involving the lending institution evaluating the company. Companies should also be evaluating the lending institution. ESOPs are term loans. The lender will be an important business partner for at least several years. Companies are well advised to seek out the lending institution they feel would be the best business partner for the foreseeable future. Some "due diligence" questions companies might consider asking lenders include:

1. What is the financial institution's stability? This is *very* important. A decline in a lending institution's financial performance is often followed by a change in lending strategy and tighten-

ing of underwriting guidelines. A highly leveraged loan that was acceptable when the transaction closed may be considered too risky under a new analysis structure, particularly if the company's financial performance deviates from forecasts.

2. Has the lending institution recently been acquired, or is it a potential acquisition target? Mergers and acquisitions bring change in management and can bring a change in loan underwriting guidelines.

3. Are there any management or strategic changes anticipated at the lending institution that would affect its credit policy?

4. Who will be the company's relationship manager going forward? Relationship managers (RMs) are the primary advocates for the company at the lending institution. RMs promote the company inside the bank. The company benefits from a long-term relationship with an RM who understands both ESOPs and the particular business.

5. How long has the lender been active in the company's market niche (size of company, size of transaction, ESOPs, industry, geographical location, deal structure, etc.)?

6. What is the likelihood of continued service by that lender to that market niche?

7. Has the company met senior management at the lending institution?

8. Does the company know how the loan approval process works? "Surprises" can be avoided by thorough due diligence on the prospective lending institution by the company.

Insufficient Collateral

It is in both the company's and lender's best interest to first provide for all credit required for ongoing operations, both revolver and term ("normal debt"). The loan value of corporate assets often does not cover both normal debt requirements *and* the proposed ESOP loan. Lenders need to be creative in structuring the transaction to best meet the seller's objectives without compromising the financial stability of the company. Table 5-6 above, which is repeated below, depicts this situation.

TABLE 5-6 (repeated). *Example of an ESOP Term Loan Creating a Collateral Shortfall.*

Asset	Gross Value	Advance Rate	Loan Value
Accounts receivable	$10,000,000	80%	$ 8,000,000
Inventory	$ 5,000,000	50%	2,500,000
Real estate	$ 5,000,000	70%	3,500,000
Fixed assets	$ 8,000,000	50%	4,000,000
Total loan value of collateral			$ 18,000,000
Less: existing revolver and term debt requirements			(10,000,000)
Collateral available for ESOP term loan			$ 8,000,000
Less: ESOP term loan			(20,000,000)
Collateral shortfall			$(12,000,000)

Overcoming this problem: In the example above, the financing question is how to structure the $12 million collateral shortfall. Creative structuring can often overcome a shortfall in the loan value of corporate assets. Ideas that have been successfully implemented include:

- *Having management investment in the transaction:* Management can invest directly, guarantee, or provide some sort of credit enhancement to bridge a financing gap. A benefit of this strategy is that it offsets the ESOP's inability to motivate key management employees. As a nondiscriminatory plan, the ESOP allocates to participants pro rata based on payroll, with a cap for highly compensated employees. This precludes key management from accumulating a disproportionate ownership stake. The downside of this strategy is that key managers often do not have significant outside net worth to provide a meaningful initial equity investment in the company.

- *Conversion of existing plan assets into employer securities:* Sometimes companies have been matching a 401(k) plan or providing attractive pension or profit sharing benefits to their employees for a number of years. Where significant plan balances have accumulated, particularly when the assets in the plan have accumulated as a result of employer contributions, it is possible to reinvest a small portion of the balances from existing plan investments into employer securities, i.e., the ESOP. In the example above with the $12 million collateral shortfall, if the company had $40 million in 401(k) balances and $10 million of the $40 million were a result of the company match, it would not be unreasonable to consider the conversion of existing plan assets for a $5 million investment in the transaction. Though this does not completely fill the $12 million requirement, lenders are comforted by the employees' conviction in their company. Perhaps the lender could then feel comfortable holding an unsecured position for the remaining $7 million. Table 5-10 depicts how the transaction works. Note: Conversion of existing plan assets into employer securities entails careful consideration of a number of important ERISA as well as possible securities law issues and benefit issues. Companies must consult with experienced benefits counsel to verify the applicability of conversion to their particular plans. Very rarely can more than a small percentage of plan assets be safely transferred.

TABLE 5-10. *Funding Example Using Conversion of Plan Assets.*

Source of Funds for Seller	Amount
Secured by corporate assets	$ 8,000,000
"Undersecured" senior debt	7,000,000
Total senior ESOP financing	$15,000,000
Conversion of existing plan assets	5,000,000
Total funds to seller	$20,000,000

- *Use of seller notes:* The seller could choose to take proceeds from the ESOP in the form of a seller note (table 5-11). For example, using the $20 million ESOP loan request above, the seller could take a note for $6 million and perhaps negotiate with the lender to provide the additional $6 million on an undersecured basis. Benefits of seller notes include attractive interest rates to the seller (they are typically subordinated to bank debt and thereby earn a market rate of about 14%) and avoidance of a mezzanine and/

or outside equity investor in the transaction. There are creative investment strategies the seller can use to enjoy the tax deferral of the Section 1042 benefit on all the sales proceeds, including subordinated notes (also see the day loan discussion under "Larger Deals" above).

TABLE 5-11. *Funding Example Using Seller Notes.*

Source of Funds for Seller	Amount
Secured by corporate assets	$ 8,000,000
"Undersecured" senior debt	6,000,000
Total senior ESOP financing	$14,000,000
Subordinated seller note	6,000,000
Total funds to seller	$20,000,000

- *Pledging of 1042 assets as collateral:* Issues and opportunities related to the pledge of 1042 assets as collateral are detailed in detail above under "The Role of Section 1042 Proceeds in Credit Structure."

- *Mezzanine and equity financing:* A third party could provide subordinated debt or equity to bridge the gap between senior financing available and total financing requirements for a particular transaction. Financial advisors are helpful in sourcing mezzanine and equity investors whose investment strategy would fit with the particular company and in resolving the related equity allocation issues associated. This details of this type of financing are beyond the scope of this chapter.

- *Cash flow financing:* Some lenders will "underwrite" a company's cash flow, essentially providing debt in excess of the loan value of assets. A cash flow lender, in the above example, would provide the entire $20 million loan request if the credit met the particular lender's underwriting standards for such loans. General guidelines for "eligibility" for cash flow lending include:
  — Stable historical revenues and margins (preferably in a non-cyclical industry).
  — Minimum of three to five years in business.
  — Revenues in excess of $20 million.

- EBITDAE in excess of $2 million.
- A senior debt to EBITDAE ratio of less than 3x. (This particular ratio changes from time to time with the expansion and contraction of the credit markets. It is also subject to change within particular lending institutions.)
- The loan should be amortized down to at or below the loan value of the borrower's assets by the end of the fourth year.

- *Second lien/junior secured:* To fill a gap between the senior credit rates and mezzanine rates, a new product is emerging called second lien or junior secured debt. These are lenders who will lend against the existing collateral pool at a rate approximately halfway between senior rates and mezzanine rates.
- *Lease financing:* Leasing companies will often advance a higher advance rate against fixed assets than traditional lenders. Another reason to look into lease financing is that there may be an opportunity to do off-balance-sheet financing at a lower cost. For example, S corporations do not need depreciation expense. Therefore, if they pass the depreciation off to someone else in exchange for a lower financing cost, they might be better off.
- *Government credit enhancement:* State and local governments are increasingly seeing ESOPs as an effective transition vehicle to keep local jobs and tax revenue. Many states have provided credit enhancements to the senior lenders to entice them to lend more to an ESOP situation. Check with your local government's economic development office.
- *High yield debt:* Depending on market conditions, ESOP companies have successfully accessed the public marketplace as a source of cash for the transaction.

Inability to Provide Cash Flow Financing

One solution to insufficient collateral is to structure the loan as a "cash flow" loan. The total credit facilities exceed the loan value of the collateral by some multiple of cash flow, depending on the strength of the credit. Some financial institutions are not interested in the credit risk associated with cash flow lending, regardless of how well structured.

Overcoming this problem: The simplest solution is to seek out a lending institution that has a "leveraged finance" division familiar with cash flow lending. Basically, leveraged finance lenders consider a company's primary asset to be that company's ability to predictably generate cash flow. This differs from an "asset-based" approach, which evaluates debt capacity based on the loan value of unencumbered corporate assets. Covenants monitor EBITDAE (earnings before interest taxes depreciation, amortization, and employee benefit expense related to the ESOP) versus tangible net worth. Unfortunately, many ESOP transactions are too small to fit the target profile of the leveraged finance units of major money center banks. Nonetheless, a company can often successfully negotiate (depending an market conditions) 12 to 24 months' cash flow "overadvance" from lenders who perhaps are not technically "leveraged finance" or "cash flow" lenders. The ability to do this was assumed in both the "seller note" and "conversion of plan assets" examples above. Companies need a solid financial plan, sensitizing revenues, and earnings to get the lender comfortable in taking on the cash flow risk.

Unique Applications

Regulated Industries

The accounting treatment for ESOPs can preclude their viability for some companies in regulated industries. "Positive net worth" is a common regulatory requirement. Nonetheless, many companies in regulated industries have successfully implemented ESOPs. Some structuring ideas a company may consider include:

- Do a smaller transaction up front that will not violate balance sheet requirements imposed by the regulators.
- Negotiate with the regulators regarding the particularities of ESOP accounting, asking them to consider "Net worth prior to adjustment for ESOP" instead of "Net worth."
- Make the loan to a holding company with the operating subsidiary meeting regulatory requirements.
- Structure the ESOP debt to the ESOT with a collateralized guarantee from the holding company.

- Be creative about "push down" accounting issues. Both the holding company and loan-to-the-ESOT strategies can be implemented to mitigate this.

- Network with the NCEO and/or the ESOP Association for names of other companies within the industry and/or professionals who have successfully implemented ESOPs with similar situations.

Union Deals

Generally, the existence of a union does not preclude a company's ability to do an ESOP. Union employees may be included in or excluded from the ESOP benefit. There are complex legal issues involved with bringing unions into an ESOP, but these are not the subject of this chapter. For example, a company may increase its cash flow, and hence its debt capacity, through contractual wage concessions on the part of the employees. In return for the value of the wage concessions, the employees receive a percentage of the ownership through an ESOP. The increased cash flow as a result of the contractual wage concessions improves the company's debt capacity, making it more attractive for lenders. There are several investment banking and legal firms that specialize in structuring these types of transactions. They can be reached via the NCEO or the ESOP Association.

Service Companies

Professional service firms are generally difficult to finance because of the lack of tangible assets. With the exception of accounts receivable, the firm's primary asset, its people, walk out the door every night. An ESOP is an excellent ownership transition vehicle for these firms. More and more professional service firms are taking advantage of employee ownership. The credit request typically needs to be evaluated on a cash flow basis per the guidelines and examples above. The main difference is that the credit markets have a "total debt to cash flow" multiple that is slightly more conservative for service companies than for asset rich non-service companies. For example, if the market senior debt multiple (total senior debt as a multiple of EBITDAE) is in the 4.0x to 4.25x range, then a service company might expect credit available in the range of 3x to 3.25x EBITDAE. This general market "contraction" in credit for professional service companies is somewhat offset by the pretax nature of the ESOP debt repayments. Be mindful that lending multiples are market-driven and vary greatly over time. Your local lender should be able to provide you with both current and historical data to educate you on current market conditions. To the extent the lender is familiar with ESOPs and comfortable with the company, a service company may enjoy the same lending multiples as the general market.

A creative way to structure a service company ESOP is to employ a combination of the strategies outlined under "Insufficient Collateral" above. The following is an example:

The owners of a professional services company (a marketing firm) valued at $40 million wanted to sell 100% of the company to an ESOP. The company had an existing revolving line of credit for working capital that they would need to increase to $20 million for a total credit request of $60 million. Positive credit attributes include:

- $17.5 million TTM (trailing twelve months) EBITDAE
- EBITDAE expected to grow 15% per year
- The ratio of funded debt (amount borrowed at closing) to EBITDAE projected at less than 3x
- Revolver fully secured by accounts receivable
- Excellent management team
- Excellent market niche
- Excellent reputation with vendors and customers
- Equity incentive for key management

An experienced ESOP cash flow lender would likely underwrite the above transaction, even though the firm is a professional services company. The committed amount of debt to historical EBITDAE is 3.4x ($60 million ÷ $17.5 million), perhaps on the high end for a service firm. However, total "unsecured" debt is 2.3 times historical EBITDAE ($40 million ÷ $17.5 million). These ratios will improve as the debt is paid down *even if the company never achieves the revenue and earnings growth projected.* The revenue and earnings growth provides the "cushion" to give a senior lender comfort on the soundness of this transaction. The facilities (revolver and term) would likely be cross-collateralized and cross-defaulted.

Further, it is common in leveraged finance and cash flow transactions to have a "cash flow recapture" provision whereby the lender requires a certain percentage of earnings after scheduled debt payment and taxes to be applied as a "prepayment" or acceleration of scheduled principal payments with the proceeds. Following the above example, if the company actually earned $21 million EBITDAE (a little bit better than its projected 15% increase) in the year following the ESOP, the cash flow recapture provision (mandatory prepayment on cash flow loans) could range from $2.4 million to $3.6 million. A 50% cash flow recapture is the norm, and 75% is not unusual, particularly in early phases on highly leveraged deals (table 5-12). 100% cash flow recapture provisions are extremely rare. Companies need to build cash for growth in working capital, capital expenditures, and so on.

TABLE 5-12. *Cash Flow Recapture.*

Income Statement	Amount
EBITDAE	$21,000,000
ESOP payment ($40,000,000 term loan – 5-year amortization)	(8,000,000)
Interest expense	(5,000,000)
Earnings before taxes	$ 8,000,000
Taxes (40% tax rate)	(3,200,000)
Funds available for recapture	$ 4,800,000
Prepayment for a 75% recapture provision	$ 3,600,000
Prepayment for a 50% recapture provision	$ 2,400,000

Construction and Engineering Companies

Though very similar to professional service firms, the growing trend of ESOPs with construction and engineering firms warrants additional detail. Construction firms are capital-intensive service companies. Many of the best firms already have sophisticated profit sharing and management incentive contracts in place to reward outstanding performance. Employee ownership is almost a natural transition for these companies. The ESOP can be structured to respect the credit requirements of bonding and insurance companies. Particularly due to the asset-intensive nature of these companies, they benefit greatly from the S corporation tax shield because all debt, not just the ESOP debt, becomes pretax debt.

Government Reimbursement

ESOPs provide an attractive ownership transition strategy for government contractors. The ESOP can have incomparable cash flow advantages compared to other opportunities. Structured appropriately, the employee benefit/ESOP debt payment can be all or partially reimbursed under existing contracts. Therefore, not only does the contractor enjoy the tax preference of repaying debt "above the line" as an "employee benefit expense," but that expense is reimbursed by the terms and conditions of its contracts as part of employee benefits and/or overhead. The lender needs to then "underwrite" the continued reimbursability of the expense. The inability to get an opinion that the expense will always be reimbursed will likely result in a lower multiple of total debt to EBITDAE (probably not to exceed 3x). The more conservative credit structure, defined by lower leverage, gives the lender the necessary cushion to lend to this type of a service company. *Note: this paragraph discusses ESOP applications from only the credit perspective with government defense contractors. The complex, IRS, legal, and ERISA considerations cannot be understated and are not addressed here.*

Spin-off/MBO/Privatization

ESOPs have also been used as the financing vehicle to spin off noncore subsidiaries from public or private companies, privatize public companies, or accomplish a management buyout of a company. These are examples that are not motivated by the Section 1042 benefit. In fact, there is no 1042 element in these examples because the Section 1042 tax deferral is not available to sellers that are C corporations. The "problem" with financing these transactions is that they are typically 100% deals. With a Section 1042 deal, the pledge of 1042 assets is one way to mitigate the leverage risk resulting from a 100% deal. The credit issue in these transactions becomes how to bridge the gap between what can be financed on a normal senior basis and what the purchase price is. Stated simply, companies are typically valued between five and eight times earnings. Senior debt, secured or unsecured, usually does not exceed four times earnings and hardly ever reaches five times earnings. Ideas that have been successfully implemented include the following (see the section above on "Insufficient Collateral" for more detail):

- Having an MBO component to the transaction: Management can invest directly, guarantee, or provide some sort of credit enhancement to bridge a financing gap.
- Conversion of existing plan assets as "equity" into the transaction.
- Note from the corporate seller.
- Mezzanine and equity financing.
- State and local government credit enhancement.

Nonleveraged ESOPs

ESOPs do not have to be leveraged. Employee ownership can be achieved without incurring debt. A closely held business owner can sell shares of stock to an ESOP over time. Figure 5-5 depicts how a seller might sell shares through annual cash contributions by the company to the ESOP. (Note: proceeds from sale of stock to an ESOP are eligible for deferral of capital gains only if the ESOP owns at least 30% of the stock of the company after the sale.)

A nonleveraged ESOP could also be implemented through annual stock contributions directly to the ESOP, as shown in figure 5-6. If the stock contributed to the ESOP consists of newly issued shares, the ownership interests of existing shareholders will be diluted.

Conclusion

ESOP loans can be extraordinarily complex, or they can be remarkably similar to any other senior term loan. The ability to successfully seek out, structure, and design a leveraged ESOP is limited only by the knowledge and creativity of the professional advisors to the transaction. The ideas and strategies presented in this chapter can serve as a springboard to think differently about financing possibilities for leveraged ESOPs. By combining thorough knowledge about

Figure 5-5. Non-Leveraged ESOP That Purchases Existing Shares

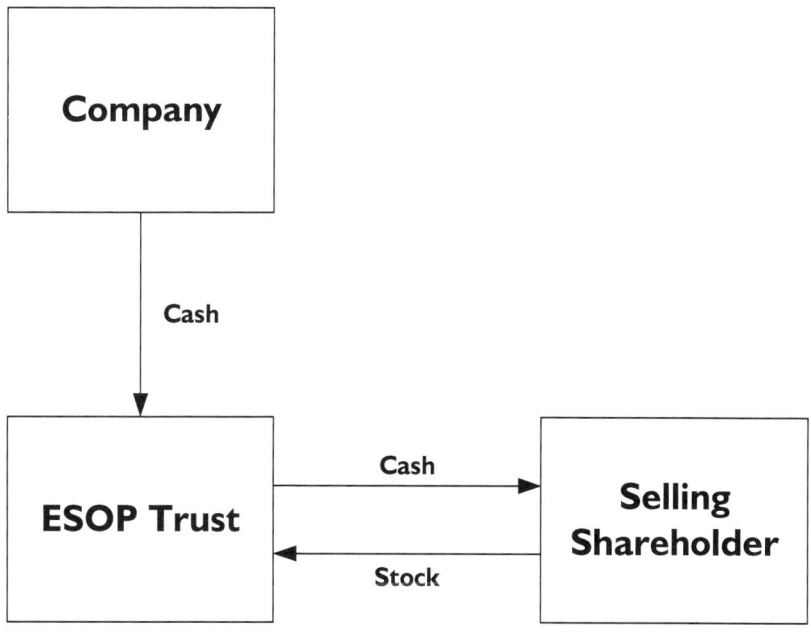

Figure 5-6. Non-Leveraged ESOP Using Stock Contributions

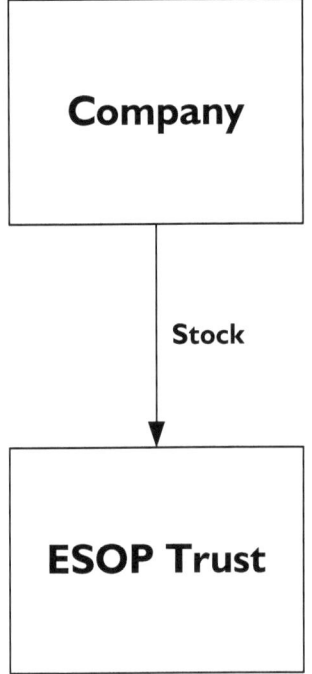

the unique characteristics of ESOPs with creative underwriting strategies, the perceived complexities can become opportunities, not deal-killers.

Appendix: Capital Markets Terminology

Best Efforts: A method of syndicating (see below) a loan facility through which one lender agrees to place as much of a debt facility as possible with other lenders under the agreed-to terms. The borrower retains risk that the deal, as contemplated, will be syndicated to an acceptable number of other lenders.

Club Deal: A bank financing involving three or more banks in which no single bank takes a formal lead in structuring the transaction. Rather, in a club deal, all of the banks work together to structure a mutually acceptable financing package for the benefit of the borrower.

Firm Underwriting: An underwriting in which a lender commits to fund an entire debt facility, bearing a syndication risk related to the financing (i.e., taking the risk that it will be able to find other lenders to purchase part of its position as a lender in a given financing). Typically, facilities of this type have higher fees and interest rates than those under club deals or best-efforts syndications.

High-Yield Bond: A bond with a speculative credit rating of BB (S&P) or Ba (Moody's) or lower. Junk or high-yield bonds offer investors higher yields than bonds of financially sound companies. Two agencies, Standard & Poors and Moody's Investor Services, provide the rating systems for companies' credit.

Institutional Lenders: Entities such as investment companies or funds, mutual funds, insurance companies, pension funds, and endowments with large amounts of capital to invest in unrelated businesses.

Junk Bond: A bond with a speculative credit rating of BB (S&P) or Ba (Moody's) or lower. Junk or high-yield bonds offer investors higher yields than bonds of financially sound companies. Two agencies, Standard & Poors and Moody's Investor Services, provide the rating systems for companies' credit.

Pro Rate Lender: A lender that purchases a fixed percentage of all tranches of a company's senior debt, including the revolver and all term loans.

Syndicate: A group of senior banks that together fund a borrower's senior debt facilities. By syndicating a transaction, lenders reduce their exposure from losses to any given borrower.

Term A: A term loan, typically from a bank, requiring interest payments and principal amortization (typically over a five- to seven-year period).

Term B: A term loan from a bank or other financial institution requiring interest payments and modest principal amortization while Term A loans are being amortized. Term B loans will typically amortize rapidly in the two years following the scheduled repayment of the Term A loan.

Chapter 6

Valuation Issues in Leveraged ESOPs

Richard C. May, Robert L. McDonald, and David C. Light

This chapter addresses the underlying economic impact of an employee stock ownership plan (ESOP) both on the value of the firm and on the value of claims held by employees through the ESOP and by other investors. Our purpose is to present consistent economic models of the impact of an ESOP on various investors versus no ESOP. It is essential for employees, their advisors, and other investors participating in ESOPs to understand fully the impact that ESOPs have on firm value and the value to third-party investors.

To accomplish this, we present economic models of ESOPs in both C corporations and S corporations. For a C corporation ESOP, the model treats the economic impact of the principal deduction[1] and the tax-free rollover[2] on shareholder value of a leveraged ESOP. First, we present an economic theory of the firm's value with a leveraged ESOP, which considers the above tax treatments. Next, we give examples of how the leveraged ESOP's value-enhancing tax treatment affects specific transactions. In addition to the C corporation leveraged ESOP, we also address the issues of valuing S corporation ESOP shares and how the special tax advantages of this ESOP form affects the value held by the ESOP trust. Finally, we address the fairness issues that arise in a sale or going-public transaction involving S corporation ESOPs.

Preliminary Valuation Considerations

The Value of the Firm[3]

The equity value of the company is the market value of the assets less any after-tax compensation claims and debt claims. The market value of all of the firm's assets (both tangible and intangible) can be derived by valuing all of the cash flows that can ultimately be derived from those assets, and then allocating the total firm value among the claimants. To analyze the effects of an ESOP, we treat employee compensation as a separate claim on the firm's assets. Equation 1 in note 3 presents the impact of compensation claims.

Table 6-1, the Base Case example, portrays the value of the equity of ABC Company derived from the cash flows produced by the firm's assets. These cash flows were projected immediately before an ESOP was installed. The pre-ESOP compensation claims of employees are included in the "Cost of Goods Sold" and "Selling, General, and Administrative Expenses" lines in table 6-1. Therefore, the value calculations of the Base Case already have employees' claims deducted.

The Value of Debt[4]

Before considering the ESOP, we will examine the pure value of leverage. This is necessary since one focus of this chapter is on gains generated by an ESOP net of gains that could have been obtained from financing techniques using conventional debt. Suppose that a firm issues conventional (i.e., non-ESOP) debt, and further assume this debt is default-free. What is the increase in total firm value (debt plus equity) from issuing this additional conventional debt?

Note 5 analyzes this question. Essentially, since lenders will hold taxable debt in place of tax-exempt debt only if they are compensated for the extra taxes they must pay, a borrower's value increases with additional debt as long as the borrower's tax rate, T, is greater than the lender's tax rate, u. To focus on the value added by the ESOP, we assume that $T = u$, so that the addition of any ordinary debt adds no value to the firm.

Valuing Firms with Leveraged ESOPs

The Firm with a Leveraged ESOP[5]

Setting up an ESOP entails transferring resources from existing stockholders to employees. The ESOP may also provide tax benefits, thereby increasing the firm's total value. The effect of the ESOP on the wealth of existing shareholders therefore depends on (1) how the ESOP affects the total resources divided between employees and

Valuation Issues in Leveraged ESOPs

TABLE 6-1. Base Case: Pre-ESOP (monetary amounts are in $000's).

	Income Statement				
	Year End Dec-04	Year Dec-05	Year Dec-06	Year Dec-07	Year Dec-08
Net Sales	$98,400	$105,000	$99,000	$105,524	$112,478
Cost of Goods Sold	(65,436)	(74,067)	(69,835)	(74,437)	(79,919)
Gross Profit	32,964	30,933	29,165	31,087	32,559
Selling, General, and Administrative Expenses	(8,462)	(9,450)	(8,910)	(9,497)	(10,123)
Operating Income	24,502	21,483	20,255	21,590	22,436
Interest Expenses	0	0	0	0	0
Income Before ESOP, Principal, and Taxes	24,502	21,483	20,255	21,590	22,436
ESOP Principal Contributions	0	0	0	0	0
Income Before Taxes	24,502	21,483	20,255	21,590	22,436
Federal and State Income Tax (39.5%)	(9,678)	(8,486)	(8,001)	(8,528)	(8,862)
Net Income	14,824	12,997	12,255	13,062	13,574
EBITDA	27,946	25,017	23,314	24,648	25,790

	Unleveraged Free Cash Flow ("UFCF")				
	Year End Dec-04	Year Dec-05	Year Dec-06	Year Dec-07	Year Dec-08
Net Income	$14,824	$12,997	$12,255	$13,062	$13,574
After-tax Interest Expenses (Tax Adjusted)	0	0	0	0	0
Unleveraged Net Income	14,824	12,997	12,255	13,062	13,574
Depreciation and Amortization	3,444	3,534	3,059	3,058	3,354
Increase in Deferred Taxes	839	632	297	147	79
Investment in Working Capital	(900)	(717)	(600)	(564)	(771)
Investment in Fixed Assets	(4,500)	(4,300)	(4,000)	(3,500)	(3,354)
Unleveraged Operating Free Cash Flow	$13,707	$12,146	$11,011	$12,203	$12,882
Unleveraged Equity Discount Rate	16%	16%	16%	16%	16%
Discounted Value of UFCF	$11,816	$9,027	$7,054	$6,740	$6,133

existing shareholders, and (2) how the ESOP affects the total compensation of employees. We will break this discussion into two parts, one on C corporation ESOPs and one on the tax benefits of S corporation ESOPs that are materially different than those of C corporation ESOPs.

To judge the fairness of the ESOP transaction from its underlying economics, we must know how the ESOP affects the size of the economic pie and also how the pie is cut after the ESOP is in place.

Suppose that the firm issues ESOP debt, existing shareholders sell common stock to the ESOP, and existing compensation is reduced dollar-for-dollar by the annual benefit to ESOP participants. The value of the firm to the pre-ESOP shareholders is its gross-of-compensation value, less after-tax compensation (adjusted for the new, lower compensation expense), plus the borrowing proceeds, less the present value of the repayment of borrowing proceeds (principal plus interest), less the value of shares given to the ESOP. Equation 5 in note 5 displays this formula. The net increase in firm value to the pre-ESOP shareholders is simplified in equation 7 in note 5, which represents (1) the gain from reduced taxes paid by the firm from the principal deductibility net of employee benefit giveups and (2) the loss to the firm from the net increase in employee compensation (the benefit of the ESOP less employee giveups).

To understand the implications of these concepts, we will present two cases, one with a full compensation offset for ESOP contributions and one with no compensation offset for ESOP contributions. However, we shall first establish a Base Case firm value with no ESOP for comparison (table 6-1).

To estimate value, a discounted cash flow methodology is used. To reflect numerically the effects of leveraged ESOPs on the value of a firm and claims on that value, we have prepared hypothetical examples based on a real transaction.

These examples highlight the effects of leverage on value determination. The business that installed an ESOP is a capital-intensive manufacturing concern whose historical operating ratios were used in determining its future financial performance. The company's growth is moderate throughout the five-year period of the projection.

These examples use an unleveraged rate of return, or discount rate, for each future period shown on the unleveraged equity discount rate in each example. This discount rate represents the discount to be applied to future net free cash flows for a marketable minority ownership interest in the firm. A marketable minority interest value is the standard used for comparison of all shareholder claims, including the ESOP's.

Base Case Firm Value Table 6-1, summarized in table 6-1a below, shows the value of the firm before the leveraged ESOP transaction.[6] The unleveraged operating free cash flows are calculated by eliminating the effects of all debt transactions from the firm's operating cash flows. The unleveraged operating free cash flows are then discounted back to their present value by the unleveraged cost of equity discount rate. Tables 6-2 and 6-3 are based on this model.

TABLE 6-1a. *Base Case Value (monetary amounts are in $000's except for per-share figures).*

Present Value of Unleveraged Firm	$105,781
Present Value of ESOP Tax Shields	0
Firm Value	105,781
Capital Debt	0
Equity Value	105,781
Divided by Voting Common Shares Outstanding	10,000
Equity Value per Share	$10,578

Tables 6-2 and 6-3 illustrate the effects of a 35% sale of the firm to the ESOP on December 31, 2003. The transaction is wholly leveraged. The selling price is assumed to be market-related, based on the pre-ESOP transaction equity value of $105.7 million calculated in table 6-1.

The Effect on Valuation of a Full Compensation Offset for ESOP Contributions Suppose that ordinary compensation (e.g., direct wages, salaries, commissions, bonuses, and benefits) is reduced dollar-for-dollar by the value of ESOP principal contributions. If this occurs, existing shareholders are indifferent about the terms of the ESOP. This makes sense: if compensation is reduced by one dollar for every dollar of net equity given to the ESOP, existing shareholders are unaffected by the ESOP, except for tax benefits.

To show how this affects the determination of firm value and the value of shareholder claims, table 6-2, summarized in table 6-2a, illustrates the effects of full compensation giveups. The compensa-

TABLE 6-2. *Post-ESOP with Full Employee Giveups (monetary amounts are in $000's).*

	Income Statement				
	Year End Dec-04	Year Dec-05	Year Dec-06	Year Dec-07	Year Dec-08
Net Sales	$98,400	$105,000	$99,000	$105,524	$112,478
Cost of Goods Sold	(65,436)	(74,067)	(69,835)	(74,437)	(79,919)
Employee Giveups	5,289	5,289	5,289	5,289	5,289
Gross Profit	38,253	36,222	34,454	36,376	37,848
Selling, General, and Administrative Expenses	(8,462)	(9,450)	(8,910)	(9,497)	(10,123)
Operating Income	29,791	26,772	25,544	26,879	27,725
Interest Expenses	(2,592)	(2,221)	(1,851)	(1,481)	(1,111)
Income Before ESOP, Principal, and Taxes	27,199	24,551	23,693	25,398	26,614
ESOP Principal Contributions	(5,289)	(5,289)	(5,289)	(5,289)	(5,289)
Income Before Taxes	21,910	19,262	18,404	20,109	21,325
Federal and State Income Tax (39.5%)	(8,655)	(7,608)	(7,270)	(7,943)	(8,423)
Net Income	13,256	11,653	11,135	12,166	12,902
	Unleveraged Free Cash Flow ("UFCF")				
	Year End Dec-04	Year Dec-05	Year Dec-06	Year Dec-07	Year Dec-08
Net Income	$13,256	$11,653	$11,135	$12,166	$12,902
After-tax Interest Expenses (tax adjusted)	1,568	1,344	1,120	896	672
After-tax ESOP Principal	3,200	3,200	3,200	3,200	3,200
Unleveraged Net Income	18,024	16,197	15,454	16,262	16,774
Depreciation and Amortization	3,444	3,534	3,059	3,058	3,354
Increase in Deferred Taxes	839	632	297	147	79
Investment in Working Capital	(900)	(717)	(600)	(564)	(771)
Investment in Fixed Assets	(4,500)	(4,300)	(4,000)	(3,500)	(3,354)
Unleveraged Operating Free Cash Flow	$16,907	$15,346	$14,210	$15,403	$16,082
Unleveraged Equity Discount Rate	16%	16%	16%	16%	16%
Discounted Value of UFCF	$14,575	$11,405	$9,104	$8,507	$7,657
ESOP Principal plus Interest Contributions	$7,881	$7,510	$7,140	$6,770	$6,400
ESOP Principal Tax Shield	$3,113	$2,967	$2,820	$2,674	$2,528
Present Value of Tax Shield	$2,684	$2,205	$1,807	$1,477	$1,204

Valuation Issues in Leveraged ESOPs

TABLE 6-3. Post-ESOP with No Employee Giveups (monetary amounts are in $000's).

	Income Statement				
	Year End Dec-04	Year Dec-05	Year Dec-06	Year Dec-07	Year Dec-08
Net Sales	$98,400	$105,000	$99,000	$105,524	$112,478
Cost of Goods Sold	(65,436)	(74,067)	(69,835)	(74,437)	(79,919)
Employee Giveups	0	0	0	0	0
Gross Profit	32,964	30,933	29,165	31,087	32,559
Selling, General, and Administrative Expenses	(8,462)	(9,450)	(8,910)	(9,497)	(10,123)
Operating Income	24,502	21,483	20,255	21,590	22,436
Interest Expenses	(2,592)	(2,221)	(1,851)	(1,481)	(1,111)
Income Before ESOP, Principal, and Taxes	21,910	19,262	18,404	20,109	21,325
ESOP Principal Contributions	(5,289)	(5,289)	(5,289)	(5,289)	(5,289)
Income Before Taxes	16,621	13,973	13,115	14,820	16,036
Federal and State Income Tax (39.5%)	(6,565)	(5,519)	(5,180)	(5,854)	(6,334)
Net Income	10,056	8,453	7,935	8,966	9,702
	Unleveraged Free Cash Flow ("UFCF")				
	Year End Dec-04	Year Dec-05	Year Dec-06	Year Dec-07	Year Dec-08
Net Income	$10,056	$8,453	$7,935	$8,966	$9,702
After-tax Interest Expenses (tax adjusted)	1,568	1,344	1,120	896	672
After-tax ESOP Principal	3,200	3,200	3,200	3,200	3,200
Unleveraged Net Income	14,824	12,997	12,255	13,062	13,574
Depreciation and Amortization	3,444	3,534	3,059	3,058	3,354
Increase in Deferred Taxes	839	632	297	147	79
Investment in Working Capital	(900)	(717)	(600)	(564)	(771)
Investment in Fixed Assets	(4,500)	(4,300)	(4,000)	(3,500)	(3,354)
Unleveraged Operating Free Cash Flow	$13,707	$12,146	$11,011	$12,203	$12,882
Unleveraged Equity Discount Rate	16%	16%	16%	16%	16%
Discounted Value of UFCF	$11,816	$9,027	$7,054	$6,740	$6,133
ESOP Principal plus Interest Contributions	$7,881	$7,510	$7,140	$6,770	$6,400
ESOP Principal Tax Shield	$3,113	$2,967	$2,820	$2,674	$2,528
Present Value of Tax Shield	$2,684	$2,205	$1,807	$1,477	$1,204

tion giveups eliminate any dilution in per-share value caused by the ESOP. The firm's annual total compensation base is about $18 million. The annual giveups in salaries and related benefits are approximately $5.3 million, or 29% of current compensation. The giveups can take the form of an initial one-time reduction in salary, a freeze on future salary increases, or a combination of these items.

TABLE 6-2a. *C Corporation ESOP with Full Compensation Offset (monetary amounts are in $000's except for per-share figures).*

Present Value of Unleveraged Firm	$132,408
Present Value of ESOP Tax Shields	11,144
Firm Value	143,552
Capital Debt	(37,023)
Equity Value	106,528
Divided by Voting Common Shares Outstanding	10,000
Equity Value per Share	$10,653

The Effect on Valuation of Not Having a Compensation Offset from ESOP Contributions Suppose there is no reduction in compensation when the ESOP is installed. The effects of the ESOP are clear in this case. The tax savings created from the deductibility of ESOP interest expense and debt principal payments increase the firm's total value. However, the equity given to the ESOP reduces the value of existing equity. The effect on existing shareholders depends on which is greater, as illustrated in table 6-3, summarized in table 6-3a below. Here, the value of shareholder claims is dramatically diluted from that calculated in table 6-2.

TABLE 6-3a. *C Corporation ESOP with No Compensation Offset (monetary amounts are in $000's except for per-share figures).*

Present Value of Unleveraged Firm	$105,781
Present Value of ESOP Tax Shields	11,144
Firm Value	116,925
Capital Debt	(37,023)
Equity Value	79,902
Divided by Voting Common Shares Outstanding	10,000
Equity Value per Share	$7,990

Comparison of C Versus S Corporation If instead of a C corporation, we were dealing with an otherwise identical S corporation, how would the above analysis differ? For a variety of reasons, most valuation professionals interpret the definition of fair market value to require that ESOP shares in an S corporation should be valued as if the company were still a taxpaying entity, i.e., as a C corporation.[7]

As a simple example, if we assume that the personal and corporate tax rates are equal, and that the company makes distributions sufficient for individual shareholders to pay personal taxes on their pro rata portion of corporate earnings, then the cash remaining in the S corporation after distributions would be identical to the cash remaining in the C corporation after corporate taxes. Thus, the company itself would be worth an identical amount in each situation described above. There would be only two economic impacts, one for the non-ESOP shareholder and another for the ESOP shareholder.

From the non-ESOP shareholder's perspective, the shareholder would receive a step-up in basis equal to all income allocated to his or her personal taxes based on the shareholder's pro rata ownership of the S corporation. When the shareholder sold his or her shares, capital gains taxes would be reduced because of the increased basis versus the C corporation situation. Thus, to quantify the benefit, we would need to know the holding period for each shareholder. Rather than quantify something that would be specific to each shareholder, we simply point out that this is a benefit to a non-ESOP shareholder in an S corporation.

From the ESOP's perspective, because the ESOP is a tax-exempt entity, its 35% ownership level would entitle it to 35% of the company's distributions. Depending on the plan's design, this cash could remain within the ESOP (rather than going to the government as taxes) and could therefore directly benefit the employees as a buildup in cash in their accounts. The distributions to the ESOP would equal 35% of each year's corporate taxes in each C corporation example since the company is assumed to pay out distributions sufficient to cover personal taxes (which were assumed calculated at a rate equal to corporate tax rates) (table 6-4).

Note that the present value of the ESOPs 35% of expected distributions from the S corporation are valued as if they continue into perpetuity. Also note that the per-share value has remained unchanged from the similar C corporation example (table 6-2a), but that the economic value expected by the ESOP is significantly greater

TABLE 6-4. *S Corporation ESOP with Full Compensation Offset (monetary amounts are in $000's except for per-share figures).*

Present Value of Unleveraged Firm	$132,408
Present Value of ESOP Tax Shields	11,144
Firm Value	143,552
Capital Debt	(37,023)
Equity Value	106,528
Divided by Voting Common Shares Outstanding	10,000
Equity Value per Share	$10,653
Number of Shares Held by ESOP	3,500
Value of Shares Held by ESOP (in thousands)	$37,285
Plus Present Value of 35.0% of Shareholder Distributions (=35.0% of C Corporation Taxes)	20,958
Total Value of Stock plus Present Value of the 35.0% of Distributions Expected by ESOP	$58,243

($58.2 million in this S corporation example versus $37.3 million). Even after accounting for the give-ups, the ESOP would be significantly better off in this example, while the non-ESOP shareholders would be essentially indifferent (versus the Base Case).

Summary The foregoing discussion shows that the value of an ESOP to existing shareholders generally depends on the firm's tax bracket, the debt amortization schedule, the value of equity given to employees, the extent to which employee compensation give ups offset the equity given to the employees, and whether the company is a C corporation or an S corporation. The higher the firm's tax bracket, the faster the debt amortization schedule, the less equity given to employees, and the greater the compensation offset, the greater are the benefits to the pre-ESOP shareholders from an ESOP.

The Value of Section 1042

Section 1042 of the Code allows selling C corporation shareholders to defer taxation of the gain realized on the sale of qualified employer stock to an ESOP if the proceeds from the sale are reinvested in qualified replacement property as defined by the Code. If the ESOP owns at least 30% of the company after the sale, certain holding and filing requirements are met, and certain other requirements are satisfied, then any gain realized on the sale to the ESOP will be recognized only to the extent that the amount realized on the sale exceeds the seller's cost for the qualified replacement property.[8]

A private business owner can achieve two major objectives through selling to an ESOP: (1) avoiding capital gains taxation through the Section 1042 tax-free rollover of sale proceeds; and (2) avoiding selling the stock to a third party and incurring a steep marketability discount.[9] By using the Section 1042 rollover provision, a private business owner who sells to an ESOP can defer, perhaps indefinitely, a substantial amount of taxes.

Assuming the equity value of $105.7 million from the Base Case analysis, no employee give ups, and an immediate sale in the open market in the absence of the 35% sale to the ESOP, the Section 1042 value to the shareholders can be quantified, as shown below.

Section 1042 Value in a 35% Sale to the ESOP Of the pre-ESOP transaction price of $105.7 the seller receives 35%, or $37 million. From the remaining shares the shareholder pays 65% of the loan servicing payments, or $14.6 million [65% × $37 million × (1 - 0.395) = $14.6 million]. This is the net cost of the debt service to the non-ESOP shareholder. Therefore, the selling shareholder receives $22.5 million [$37 million - $14.6 million, or 61% of $37 million].

Comparison of Section 1042 Value in ESOP to a 35% Sale to the Public (Non-ESOP) In a private sale to a non-ESOP buyer the seller must pay taxes and face a discount for lack of marketability, which we assume is 30%. Therefore, in a non-ESOP sale the selling shareholder receives $22 million [$37 million × (1 - 0.30) × (1 - 0.15), or 60% of $37 million]. A comparison of the amounts received by the selling shareholder under each scenario indicates that the shareholder receives a slightly higher proportion of the sale proceeds when using the leveraged ESOP as the financing vehicle.

Under current law, sales by shareholders of an S corporation to an ESOP do not qualify for deferral of capital gains taxes under Section 1042. Therefore, the proceeds received by a selling S corporation shareholder to an ESOP in the above example would be $16.9 million [$37 million × (1 – 0.15) – $14.6 million, or 46% of $37 million]. In this example, a sale of S corporation stock to an ESOP would net the seller the least amount of proceeds because Section 1042 would not be allowed.

Repurchase Obligation

The analysis above assumes the value of employee give-ups is approximately equal (on a present value basis) to the value of stock given to the ESOP. The company's policy regarding whether to "retire" ESOP shares after repurchase into the treasury, or to "recycle" those shares by giving them once again to employees does not alter the analysis, as long as this "retire" versus "recycle" decision was accounted for in calculating the value of employee give-ups at the time of the original ESOP transaction.

However, if an *unplanned* change in the "retire" versus "recycle" policy for ESOP shares is instituted after the transaction, then there should be an equal and opposite change in other employee compensation to balance the value impact of such a policy change. As long as total compensation is unchanged by the "retire" versus "recycle" choice, then the conclusion that an ESOP transaction produces higher after-tax proceeds to the seller than a third party sale remains valid, even after accounting for repurchase obligation effects.

S Corporation ESOPs

On January 1, 1998, corporations with ESOPs became eligible to elect S corporation tax status. As described briefly above, by becoming an S corporation, all income generated by a company is no longer taxed at the corporate level. Rather, each shareholder must include a pro rata portion of the S corporation's income in his or her tax filing, and thus each is liable for taxes on his or her share of the income at individual tax rates. The net effect is the elimination of double taxation incurred by C corporations (the corporate income tax plus the tax on dividends). For an S corporation shareholder, liquidity becomes an issue because a personal tax liability is incurred if the company earns income. Typically, an S corporation's policy is to make a cash distribution to its shareholders at least equivalent to the individual with the highest tax rate, alleviating the liquidity problem for its shareholders.

The two key provisions of the law allowing S corporation ESOPs to hold company stock are: (1) an ESOP trust is able to hold stock in an S corporation; and (2) the ESOP shareholder is not required to pay any taxes on its pro rata portion of the company's income. Therefore, while individual shareholders will use their company's cash distributions to pay personal tax liabilities associated with the S corporation's earnings, the ESOP trust can simply retain the cash or repay its debt. Additionally, S corporations can only have one class of stock, so if distributions are made to one shareholder, then pro rata distributions must be made to all shareholders.

If we assume that corporate and individual tax rates are equal and further assume all company expenses remain constant before and after the S election (including any ESOP contributions), then the increase in economic value to the ESOP due to the S election is the present value of the ESOP's pro rata portion of expected corporate income tax savings, discounted at the leveraged equity rate.[10]

From a fair market value shareholder perspective, assuming the only change is the company's tax status (S versus C), then the company's after-tax cash flows as a C corporation will be identical to its after-distribution cash flows as an S corporation. Therefore, the stock should have approximately the same value in both cases.

Because of the unique tax treatment of ESOPs in S corporations, very powerful employee benefit and corporate finance transactions can be structured. To illustrate the opportunities that an S corporation ESOP structure affords, let us return to the example of a leveraged ESOP in a C corporation. Let us assume in our C corporation example that instead of a leveraged buyout of the shareholders' 35% interest, we instead calculate the economics of an ESOP that has achieved 100% ownership and elected S corporation status.

In this case, the additional economic value to the ESOP would be the present value of all C corporation taxes that would have been paid but for the S corporation election. Using the taxes owed from each of the C corporation 35% ESOP cases, we calculate the present value of future tax savings to the ESOP assuming it instead owned 100% of an S corporation. This value could build up either as cash in the ESOP (if distributions are made) or as cash in the company).

In the case of full benefit substitution, the results are that the present value of all future taxes (and thus tax savings) is almost $60 million. If we assume no benefit substitution, the present value to participants of the 100% ESOP-owned S ownership structure would be around $33 million.

Fairness Issues in S Corporation ESOPs

As can be seen above in our examples, S corporation ESOPs can realize above-market returns for ESOP participants through the elimination of federal income taxes. However, these above-market returns are not exclusively reserved for ESOP participants. The above market returns can be shared, within the limits specified in Code Section 409(p) and the regulations thereunder, with other equity-based claimants in the S corporation. Examples would be holders of warrants or phantom stock issued by the S corporation.

This chapter is not intended to address detailed issues that arise under Section 409(p) and the regulations. What we wish to point out is that third-party investors can also benefit from the unusual tax advantages bestowed on S corporation ESOPs. To illustrate this most clearly, we will revisit our above example of a company whose common stock is 100% owned by an ESOP in an S corporation. In this example, we calculated the enhancement of value to the ESOP participants from the accumulation of S corporation distributions that normally flow to stockholders to pay federal income taxes. However, if instead of making distributions to pay taxes, which the ESOP participants have no obligation to pay, the corporation retains these distributions to pay down debt, increase cash, or invest in the growth and development of the company, the resulting value creation flows to all S corporate equity-based claimants. This will significantly enhance returns for all investors, principally the ESOP participants but also third parties, e.g., holders of phantom stock, stock appreciation rights, and warrants.

Because S corporations with ESOPs have these above-market return characteristics for their ESOP participants, any potential sale, merger, or going-public transaction raises special fairness issues for the trustee, particularly if the ESOP is in a controlling position. This can be seen directly by examining the values for the ESOP shown in tables 6-2a and 6-4 above. Comparing identical companies, one in the C corporate form and the other in S corporate form, the ESOP participants in the S corporation will (all other things being equal) always realize greater returns if the company remains an S corporation. In fact, the longer they remain in that situation, the larger the benefit becomes. How then can an S corporation controlled by an ESOP ever be sold or go public when either of these transactions would result in the termination of the federal tax forgiveness and therefore almost certainly lower expected returns for the ESOP participants?

The issue raised by the magnitude of the economic benefits that flow to the ESOP and its participants in the S corporation is one of absolute fairness. This element of a fairness opinion analyzes the present value of the hold strategy (i.e., what happens if the ESOP rejects the proposed transaction) versus the present value of a sale, merger, or going-public transaction (i.e., if the ESOP accepts the proposed transaction). Absolute fairness requires that the proposed transaction's present value meet or exceed the present value of the hold strategy. It is possible that a buyer could offer a price that matches the present value derived from ESOP's tax forgiveness, but, as can be seen from the above illustrations, that is far from certain given the expected present value of the tax forgiveness even for strategic buyers. It is also possible that in order to continue to grow, or meet emergent capital needs, or to fund the S corporation's repurchase obligation, the equity markets are the only or the most compelling solution. Our point is that once the ESOP acquires control in an S corporation, the threshold for satisfying the absolute fairness requirements of any transaction that would extinguish the tax benefits is raised materially.

Conclusion

The leveraged ESOP is one of the most powerful and yet underused ownership transition tools available to privately held American businesses. Benefits accrue to the employees and the selling shareholder or shareholders alike. These benefits are of obvious value to business owners who are astute enough to explore this transition option. They also offer compelling financial opportunities to build significant retirement accounts for the management and employees of companies that install ESOPs.

Notes

1. Internal Revenue Code ("Code") §§ 404(k) and 415(c)(6).
2. Code § 1042.
3. *The value of a firm.* To calculate the value of a firm, let W denote the value of the firm without an ESOP and gross of compensation (i.e., before compensation expense is deducted). Let pretax compensation at time t be denoted $c(t)$. The value of the firm without an ESOP and without conventional debt (denoted as V^*) is:

    EQUATION 1

    $V^* = W - (1 - T)C$

    where $C = \Sigma b^t c(t)$ is the present value of future gross-of-tax compensation expenses; b (equaling $1 \div (1 + r)$, where r equals the discount rate) is the discount factor for future cash flows; and T is the firm's tax rate. Equation 1 reflects the tax deductibility of compensation expense.

4. *The value of debt.* Suppose that a firm with total market value V issues B in default-free, non-ESOP debt. What is the increase in total firm value (debt plus equity) from issuing this debt? Suppose that lenders are taxed at the rate u and that the tax-exempt interest rate is ρ. If the rate required by investors to hold taxable debt is $i = \rho \div (1 - u)$, investors will hold taxable debt in place of tax-exempt debt only if they are compensated for the extra taxes they must pay. Let Y_t denote the debt amortization in each period (i.e., Y is the fraction of principal paid in each period), and let Γ_t denote the percentage of remaining principal in period t relative to the original total debt, B. The value of the firm with conventional debt, $V(B)$, is:

EQUATION 2

$$V(B) = V^* + B - \Sigma b^t [Y_tB + (1 - T)i\Gamma_tB] = V^* + B - \Sigma b^t [Y_tB + r[(1 - T) \div (1 - u)] \Gamma_tB].$$

To interpret the algebra, note that $\Sigma b^t Y_t B$ = the present value of principal repayments, and that $\Sigma b^t (1 - T)i\Gamma_t B$ = the present value of after-tax interest payments. To the bondholder, the NPV of debt is 0 so that Equation 3 holds:

EQUATION 3

$$B = \Sigma b^t[Y_tB + i\Gamma_tB].$$

Using this, equation 2 becomes

EQUATION 4

$$V(B) = V^* + r[(T - u) \div (1 - u)]\Sigma b^t\Gamma_tB.$$

This is the traditional analysis of the value of debt: the value of the firm is increasing in the amount of debt issued if $T > u$. To focus on the value added by the ESOP, we will assume that $u = T$, so that an ordinary debt issue adds no value to the firm.

5. *The firm with a leveraged ESOP.* Suppose that the firm issues B in ESOP debt, gives to the ESOP shares worth E, and reduces existing compensation by λE. The total increase in compensation is then $(1 - \lambda)E$. The value of the firm to the pre-ESOP shareholders is its gross-of-compensation value (W), less after-tax compensation, plus the borrowing proceeds (B), less the present value of the repayment of borrowing proceeds (principal plus interest), less the value of shares given to the ESOP (E):

EQUATION 5

$$V(B, E, \lambda) = W - (1 - T)(C - \lambda E) + B - (1 - T)\Sigma b^t[Y_tB + i\Gamma_tB] - E.$$

Under the assumption that there is no tax advantage to issuing ordinary debt ($u = T$), it follows that the present value of after-tax debt repayments (excluding the deductibility of principal repayment) equals the current value of the debt:

EQUATION 6

$B = \Sigma b^t[Y_tB + i(1 - T)\Gamma_tB]$.

Substituting equation 6 into equation 5 and rewriting gives $V(B, E, \lambda) = W - (1 - T)(C - \lambda E) + T\Sigma b^t Y_t B - E = W - (1 - T)C + T(\Sigma b^t Y_t B - \lambda E) - (1 - \lambda)E$. The value added by the ESOP to the pre-ESOP shareholders is thus:

EQUATION 7

$V(B, E, \lambda) - V^* = T(\Sigma b^t Y_t B - \lambda E) - (1 - \lambda)E$.

6. All monetary amounts in the tables are in thousands of dollars.
7. See, e.g., Kathryn F. Aschwald and Donna J. Walker, "Valuing S Corporation ESOP Companies," in *S Corporation ESOPs* (Oakland, CA: NCEO, 2004); "Valuation Issues in S Corporation ESOPs," ESOP Association Valuation Advisory Committee white paper.
8. Code § 1042.
9. ESOP stock in privately held companies tends to be more marketable than non-ESOP stock in the same companies because of ESOP participants' put right inherent in such shares upon certain events.
10. In an equation, the economic benefit to an ESOP from the S election is:

EQUATION 8

Economic Benefit to ESOP = $\Sigma (PI_i \times EO \times T) / (1 + k_e)^i$

where: PI_i = Pretax Income in Year i

EO = ESOP Ownership Percentage

T = Tax Rate

k_e = Equity Discount Rate

Chapter 7

Accounting for Employee Stock Ownership Plan Transactions

Rebecca J. Miller

Too frequently, the accountant is called into the picture after a leveraged employee stock ownership plan (ESOP) transaction has been implemented and the financing obtained. To start educating the plan sponsor on the accounting treatment of ESOPs at that late date is certain to be an unhappy experience. By that time, the transaction may be too far down the road to be able to avoid or minimize any potentially adverse accounting treatment. Many people simply do not recognize the dramatic impact that a leveraged ESOP will have on the financial statements of the plan sponsor.

The purpose of this chapter is to describe the basics of accounting for leveraged ESOP transactions so that potential plan sponsors and their advisors can anticipate the accounting presentation and restructure the transaction as necessary to minimize any complications created by the accounting. This chapter is only a primer on the rules covering the accounting for leveraged ESOPs and will not cover all of the intricacies of very sophisticated ESOP applications. Nor will it go into much detail on the accounting for nonleveraged ESOPs. ESOP sponsors or potential sponsors will still need to get their accounting firms involved in the early stages of planning.

This chapter begins with an explanation of ESOP accounting rules through 1992. In 1993, changes were made concerning compensation expenses, earnings per share (EPS), and dividend treatment, as described in the second part of the chapter. This historical perspective is necessary because the development of the financial reporting for leveraged ESOPs has evolved over time. The current rules can only be fully understood in the context of how they have developed. Also, the 1993 changes to the accounting rules included a grandfather provision for existing ESOP arrangements. Some loans covered by the old rules are still outstanding.

Background

Before describing the accounting rules in detail, it may help readers who are not accountants to understand how these rules are created. Most people have some understanding of how tax and Employee Retirement Security Act of 1974 (ERISA) regulations are written. If questioned on the accounting rules, however, those same people would have little idea of how an accounting principle is developed and what importance it has to their financial future.

Even after the recent Sarbanes-Oxley legislation, the accounting profession remains a self-regulated professional group. In an attempt to achieve uniformity, the profession establishes Generally Accepted Accounting Principles (GAAP). Most accounting standards are issued by the Financial Accounting Standards Board (FASB). FASB issues Statements of Financial Accounting Standards, referred to as FASB Statements, and FASB Interpretations, referred to simply as Interpretations. Before 2002, the next level of accounting authority was issued by the Accounting Standards Executive Committee (AcSEC) of the American Institute of Certified Public Accountants (AICPA). This group issued Statements of Position, referred to as "SOPs." An SOP does not depart from the general rules established by the FASB. Since 2002, AcSEC has only issued guidance on industry-specific accounting and auditing matters. The last group authorized to issue accounting authority is the Emerging Issues Task Force (EITF) of the FASB. This group is the least formal and is authorized only to interpret current standards. Such interpretations, however, do have the standing of GAAP. These interpretations are referred to as EITF Issues.

The FASB provides for a public comment period before they release a statement. When comments are received, the staff reviews them. Changes may be proposed in response to such comments. In any event, any standard passes in front of the applicable board or boards before final approval. If the public comments raise serious issues that result in major modifications in a proposal, a second comment period may be provided before finalizing a standard.

A FASB Interpretation can be released without any public comment but generally involves significant time in drafting. The EITF, on the other hand, can respond quite quickly. It holds approximately 10 meetings every year. If consensus can be reached at a single meeting, new GAAP may be created.

Besides these private entities, the SEC issues accounting pronouncements for public companies. These releases typically concern issues relevant to the public market. However, if there is no other GAAP pronouncement on the topic, an SEC Accounting Release may be considered to apply even to private companies. In addition, the SEC substantially influences GAAP through its participation with the FASB.

It is rare for any other entities to become involved in drafting accounting rules for the public. Within regulated industries, the regulatory agencies may require deviations from GAAP or may supplement GAAP. However, the regulatory rules are applied only in preparing statements for the regulators, not for other users who request GAAP statements.

Today, the accounting standard setters are dealing with the concept of "convergence." As more and more businesses compete in a global marketplace, the need for uniform standards across nations has become evident. To address this concept, the accounting community formed the International Accounting Standards Board (IASB).

Most users of financial statements (lenders, for example), will require that a "clean" opinion be provided by the auditor. A clean opinion is one that states that the financial statements have been subject to generally accepted auditing standards and are presented in accordance with generally accepted accounting principles with no exceptions. The failure to provide a clean opinion will reduce the amount of credence that the users will have for the statements. Because most leveraged ESOPs do involve a lender, it is important to understand how the ESOP will affect the financial statements of the plan sponsor.

Specific ESOP Accounting Authority

From 1976 until 1989, the accounting for ESOP transactions was controlled by Statement of Position 76-3, "Accounting Practices for Certain Employee Stock Ownership Plans," published by the AICPA in 1976. This was issued before the Internal Revenue Service (IRS) and the Department of Labor (DOL) had finalized their regulations governing the operation of leveraged ESOPs. This statement, referred to as SOP 76-3, was later affirmed as GAAP by Statement of Financial Accounting Standard No. 32.

At the time that SOP 76-3 was issued, because ESOPs were quite new, most of them were very simple arrangements. All of the later activity involving convertible preferred stock, debt service with deductible dividends, reduced interest loans, immediate allocation loans, and so on was not yet encouraged through special tax incentives. Therefore, most of the plans were straightforward financing and compensation devices.

In response to this, a simple accounting standard was developed. The upsurge in ESOP activity during the 1980s, however, highlighted inadequacies in the SOP. This caused a great deal of activity on the part of the FASB's Emerging Issues Task Force during 1989 to amplify and apply the terms of the SOP to the creative ESOP applications that came about because of the 1984 and 1986 tax law changes. In 1989 the EITF dealt with only 20 accounting issues, four of which were ESOP-related.

This flurry of activity caused the accounting community to rethink the existing ESOP guidance. In fall 1989, the AcSEC formed a committee to address ESOP accounting. After more than three years of meetings, public comments and hearings, a revised model for the reporting of leveraged and non-leveraged ESOPs was approved. That standard applies to shares acquired on or after December 31, 1992. A plan sponsor may elect to apply it to earlier periods, but is not required to do so. The prior accounting rules under SOP 76-3 and the numerous EITF consensus opinions may continue to be applied.

Apart from this development, a significant controversy took place during 1991 and 1992 as a result of a proposed revision of Statement of Financial Accounting Standards No. 96 (SFAS 96) dealing with the reporting of income taxes. A portion of the changes in SFAS 96 also has a significant impact on sponsors of ESOPs. The revised statement, SFAS 109, effective for 1993 with no transition rule, interacts with the new ESOP accounting standard in critical ways for sponsors that use dividends for debt service.

In addition, in the spring of 1992 the EITF issued a clarification on the treatment of the tax benefit on common shares held by an ESOP for reporting earnings per share. This is EITF Consensus Opinion 92-3. This opinion was necessary to integrate the impact of SFAS 109 and prior EITF Consensus Opinion 90-4. (Note that Consensus Opinion 90-4 applied only to preferred dividends. The impact of the tax benefit of common dividends was specifically not the subject of consensus.)

At the same time, the FASB was working on rewriting the rules for compensatory devices based upon company stock. That paper focused on stock options, but could have included ESOPs. That project was extremely controversial and resulted in no significant changes to the measurement of earnings, just additional disclosures.

Currently, the accounting profession is dealing with issues associated with securities that have some attributes of both stock and equity. This project resulted in the issuance of "Statement of Financial Accounting Standard 150—Accounting for Certain Financial Instruments with Characteristics of both Liabilities and Equity." This standard currently does not apply to ESOP transactions. However, the FASB has announced that the second phase of this project will apply to *puttable securities*, as such, ESOP sponsors must keep abreast of these developments. The FASB is also reconsidering SFAS 123 on equity compensation tools (options, etc.). A revised standard on options is to be exposed for comment in the spring of 2004. The FASB is also reconsidering SFAS 123 on equity compensation tools (stock options, etc.) as part of a comprehensive revision to the accounting for equity compensation techniques. A revised standard on equity compensation is to be exposed for comment in spring 2004. FASB has announced its intentions to take a new look at ESOP accounting when the revised standard on equity compensation is completed.

The remainder of this chapter covers how a leveraged ESOP affects the plan sponsor's financial statements. Most of this discussion focuses on the direct ESOP loan, where the ESOP borrows money directly from the lender but the plan sponsor services the debt with contributions or dividends. Perhaps more common are ESOPs established with an inside loan. Here, the plan sponsor borrows funds from an outside lender and then loans these funds to the ESOP. Where the accounting for the inside loan varies from that of the direct loan, the appropriate comments are included in the text. Other ESOP structures are discussed later in the chapter. The following discussion is for financial statement purposes only and does not bear on the income tax treatment of ESOPs.

Balance Sheet

The first financial statement presented in any official set of financial statements is the balance sheet. Generally, this has three parts: assets, liabilities, and equity. For sponsors of certain ESOPs another section, temporary equity or mezzanine capital, also may be present.

Assets

Other than the obvious increase in cash or other assets resulting from the financing aspect of the plan, an ESOP has no direct affect on the asset side of the balance sheet. The assets of the plan are not reported as assets of the sponsor. In the event that the sponsor has a note receivable from the plan because internal financing was used, that note receivable is not recorded as an asset; instead, it affects the equity section.

Liabilities

When SOP 76-3 was originally proposed, it was the ESOP's affect on the liabilities of the plan sponsor that prompted the most controversy. According to the SOP, if the plan sponsor has guaranteed or otherwise committed to fund the debt of the ESOP, that debt must be shown on the balance sheet of the plan sponsor as a direct obligation. This statement was intended to be read quite broadly. With respect to the commitment to pay, virtually any language that implies a guarantee is held to constitute such a commitment. For example, the plan might require that the sponsor make contributions sufficient to fund the debt, even if the lender has required no such commitment. Also, most accountants enforced an "implied" commitment rule. If the loan was made on the basis of the creditworthiness of the plan sponsor, not the plan's financial position, the "implied" commitment was deemed to exist and the debt would be recorded upon the financial statements of the plan sponsor.

During the late 1980s, however, it became apparent that there was an unacceptable degree of nonconformity in the interpretation of the "commitment" language. Therefore, the EITF released Issue No. 89-10, "Sponsor's Recognition of Employee Stock Ownership Plan Debt." In its consensus, the EITF decided that *all* ESOP debt is to be recorded on the balance sheet of the plan sponsor, regardless of the existence or nonexistence of any enforceable obligation of the sponsor to amortize the debt. This conclusion was based on the simple assumption that the plan sponsor is the sole source of all of the cash to be used by the ESOP for debt service. The EITF conclusion is to apply without regard to whether the debt is to be satisfied through contributions, dividends, or the sale of the securities. (With regard to using the proceeds from the sale of securities for debt service, remember that the IRS and DOL are quite conservative in interpreting when that is an allowable potential source of cash to be used to service the note.) The only exception to this recording of the debt is where an *unrelated* party has agreed to make periodic payments to service the debt. It is difficult to imagine where this might arise.

This EITF conclusion was considered to be a major change in the interpretation of SOP 76-3. Therefore, in an unusual move for the accounting profession, the application of this new interpretation was made effective for ESOP loans made after June 19, 1989, the date of the EITF meeting in which this conclusion was reached. Unlike the effective date language that is frequently contained in tax bills, there are no special qualification rules to grandfather in loans that were negotiated before this date but not closed until after this date. If the loan closed or was renegotiated after June 19, 1989, the new rule applies.

Under SOP 93-6, all ESOP debt is reflected on the financial statement of the plan sponsor. There is no potential for off balance sheet financing under the current standards.

One major, unanswered question remained after the issuance of EITF Issue 89-10: How is the debt to be reflected upon the balance sheet of a subsidiary that participates in a single plan that covers the parent corporation and some or all of the subsidiaries? In the minutes from the June 19, 1989, EITF meeting, there is a specific reference to the fact that the EITF members did not discuss this matter. Common sense would argue that if the subsidiary's employees are covered by the plan, then that subsidiary is, theoretically, benefiting from that portion of the ESOP and should reflect that portion of its debt. (That "common sense" approach, of course, assumes that it is common sense to book the debt at all, a position that many plan sponsors, but few knowledgeable accountants, argue is not sensible in the least.)

In any event, the accounting practitioner might initially argue that it makes no difference since GAAP requires a consolidated balance sheet in the case of a parent/subsidiary group. In this case, it is irrelevant where the debt is initially recorded, the parent or the subsidiary, since it all ends up in the same place. A problem arises in the case of separate financial statements of regulated enterprises (banks or savings and loan institutions, bonded warehouses, etc.) that are subsidiaries of holding companies. In these cases, the regulators or bonding companies impose rigid financial ratio requirements. These requirements affect the way the enterprise can conduct its business. Generally, however, the regulators seem to look at GAAP financial statements of the operating subsidiaries only. They do not look at any debt of the holding company when analyzing the subsidiary's ability to do business. In the past, these entities have used leveraged ESOPs at the parent company level. This has left the debt at that level and not brought it down to the operating subsidiaries. To date, disparity still exists in accounting practice on whether to "push down" this debt from the parent to one or more of the subsidiaries. As discussed under SOP 93-6, the argument against "pushdown" accounting has been weakened for post-1992 transactions. The only recommendation that can be made at this time is to discuss the matter specifically with your accountant in the event that any recording of the debt at the subsidiary level could have an adverse effect on the plan sponsor's ability to do business.

All of this discussion under "liabilities" has focused on the major issue of the recording of the ESOP loan by the sponsor. There is also an ancillary, though occasionally equally frustrating, issue. This is the recording of the current accrual for the current year's contribution to the plan. Generally, any long-term obligation will be separated annually into two pieces. These are the short-term piece, the amount that is payable in the next 12 months, and the long-term piece, the amount not payable within 12 months. The first is recorded as a current liability. The second is recorded as a long-term liability.

In most cases, where the employer makes its qualified plan contribution after the end of the year, the balance sheet will show a current liability for any unfunded amount of the accrued plan contribution. If a sponsor has a leveraged ESOP, the unfunded amount of the accrued contribution might already be recorded in current liabilities in the form of the current portion of the ESOP debt. Under SOP 76-3, until the contribution is actually made, that debt cannot be eliminated. If the current accrual for the contribution is also recorded, that portion of current debt will be reflected twice in the current liabilities section of the plan sponsor's balance sheet. It is, however, possible to reflect only one current element. That is, the current portion of the ESOP debt is shown as long term. Only the accrued contribution is shown in current liabilities. Even then, the amount of the current contribution to the plan is included twice in the liabilities section of the balance sheet. Some practitioners argue that EITF Consensus 89-10 would allow one to offset the current portion of the ESOP debt and the contra account before the actual payment is made. This avoids the double-counting of that portion of the debt, but such an interpretation is controversial.

This double-counting can be avoided by scheduling the payment to coincide with the end of the financial statement period. However, that may not be the best cash management technique because, for income tax purposes, the plan sponsor could take a tax deduction for an amount paid as late as eight and one-half months after year-end. It is also possible to minimize this by properly planning the closing date of the transaction. That way, the plan sponsor may be able to protect the cash planning attributes of the plan and the liability section. Clearly, an accountant or financial planner needs to be involved during the transaction to help measure any potential adverse consequences of this aspect of a leveraged ESOP.

This problem is eliminated under SOP 93-6; see the discussion below.

The above section covers the recording of a direct loan to the ESOP. In the more typical two-step or indirect loan transaction, the company borrows funds from another source and makes a second loan to the ESOP. Occasionally, the sponsor has the funds on hand and makes a direct loan to the ESOP. In such cases, the credit relationship between the ESOP and the sponsor is not recorded as an asset or a liability. To the extent the sponsor borrowed funds from another party, that loan, of course would be recorded.

Equity

Anyone who has had an introductory accounting course will remember that every credit entry must have an equal debit entry or the books will not balance. In booking the ESOP loan, a credit is recorded. As stated earlier, the establishment of the ESOP has no impact on assets, where debits would normally show up on the balance sheet. That leaves us with only one other place to put this dangling debit, the equity section. At the same time that the debt is recorded (or the cash is advanced for an indirect or two-step loan), an equal and offsetting debit is recorded as a single line in the equity section. This reduces the net equity. This is referred to as the "ESOP Loan Contra Account" or "Unearned Compensation." Under SOP 93-6, this contra account is called "Unearned ESOP Shares."

This contra equity account is eliminated as the ESOP debt is retired. The amount of reduction in the contra account for any year is measured by the amount of compensation expense recorded on the plan financial statements attributable to ESOP activity. In the past, this was a simple entry. Before 1989, compensation expense was measured by the contribution made by the employer during the year to amortize principal on the ESOP loan. In 1989, however, the EITF changed this method of measuring the ESOP compensation cost to one that took into account the number of shares that were released from collateral and allocated to the accounts of ESOP participants for each year. This is discussed below in more detail under "Income Statement: Development of Rules Through 1992." The important point to recognize with this entry is that it will not necessarily be reduced at the same time or in the same amount that the ESOP loan balance is reduced.

EITF Consensus Opinion 89-8 changed the measurement of compensation cost and, therefore, the adjustments to the contra account. Where the plan sponsor uses the principal-and-interest method of collateral release within the plan, the contra account will no longer reflect the mirror image of the debt. This changed again under SOP 93-6; see the discussion below.

The ESOP's impact on retained earnings is reflected in two entries: earnings and dividends. Under the pre-1993 rules, dividends paid on most ESOP shares retain their character as dividends; they are not compensation expense. (There was one, limited, exception: dividends paid on unallocated shares resulting from the transfer of a defined benefit plan excess.) As dividends, they are charged directly to retained earnings.

The tax benefit from ESOP dividends is covered by SFAS 109. All of the tax benefit runs through the tax provision. This is true whether the dividends are recorded as part of compensation cost or retain their character as dividends.

During 1989, another change was made in the manner that ESOPs may affect the equity section. This is described in EITF Issue

89-11, "Sponsor's Balance Sheet Classification of Capital Stock with a Put Option Held by an Employee Stock Ownership Plan." This issue is generally considered to apply only to publicly traded enterprises, as it is based on the interpretation of SEC Accounting Release No. 268, "Presentation in Financial Statements of Redeemable Preferred Stocks." This release effectively provides that any stock held by an ESOP that is subject to a put option is to be classified outside of permanent capital. That is, it will be recorded into the portion on the right side of the balance sheet between debt and equity. This is frequently referred to as the "mezzanine" level. According to the EITF, the proportionate share of the contra equity account attributable to these shares will also be recorded at this mezzanine level. These shares can remain in permanent equity if the plan sponsor can issue stock for the puts and has expressed the intent to do so. Any plan sponsor who makes this representation must realize that in that case, the SEC is likely to hold that the ESOP shares are common stock equivalents for purposes of calculating primary earnings per share. A key issue to understand about this mezzanine capital is that the stock is marked to market value. This is an area that may change as the FASB's work on financial instruments progresses.

Before leaving the discussion of the ESOP's affect on the equity section, it is critical to note how inside loans, sometimes referred to as mirror loans, two-step loans, or back-to-back loans, affect the equity section. A simple inside loan is one in which the plan sponsor makes the loan to the plan without obtaining any related financing from the outside. The other terms describe situations in which the plan sponsor receives financing from the outside, then in turn loans funds to the ESOP. As noted earlier, however, the note receivable represented by the inside note between the plan sponsor and the ESOP is not recorded as an asset. Instead, that note receivable is what is reflected in the contra equity account in the equity section of the balance sheet.

Impact of SOP 93-6 on Balance Sheet Presentation

Most of the comments above continue to apply under SOP 93-6. The major distinctions are:

- There is now no basis for keeping ESOP debt off the balance sheet of the plan sponsor.

- There is no double counting of an accrued contribution at year end and the current portion of the ESOP debt.
- The ESOP contra account now has a specific title, "Unearned ESOP shares."
- The contra account is reduced as shares are allocated, not necessarily as the debt is paid.
- It is more likely that the "push down" of the debt to separately reported financial statements of participating subsidiaries could be required.
- Dividends on allocated shares are charged to retained earnings.

These changes are all effective for acquisitions of securities by an ESOP after December 31, 1992. The plan sponsor may elect to apply these rules to preexisting arrangements.

Income Statement and Earnings per Share

Income Statement: Development of Rules Through 1992

When the original SOP was issued, there was as much controversy over the measurement of compensation expense as there was over the recording of the debt. Basically, both controversies revolved around the same issue: Is the ESOP a compensation device, a financing device, or both? The accounting community is still wrestling with this issue. However, in publishing SOP 76-3, the AcSEC had made the decision that it is both. Therefore, the income statement impact of an ESOP reflects a compensation cost and an interest cost. That basic conclusion continues to apply under the current accounting rules. (For purposes of this chapter, compensation expense and interest expense are discussed as though they are currently deductible. Any issues pertaining to whether some or all of one or the other need to be capitalized are outside of the scope of this discussion.)

There is no magic to the measurement of the interest expense. It is measured in the same manner as it would be for any other similar financial instrument.

The measurement of the compensation element is another story. Initially, when the SOP was issued and through December 1989, the common interpretation of the SOP was that compensation expense was to be measured by the amount of principal paid each year to amortize the loan. This was consistent with the world of ESOP loans that were in existence in 1976 when the SOP was issued. It also is consistent with the income tax reporting.

At that time, ESOP lending was in its infancy, and the sophistication of the loans was limited. The regulations interpreting the new law were not even available, so most ESOP lenders made classic commercial loans to these plans. These required either equal periodic payments of principal and interest or equal periodic payments of principal, plus accrued interest. Therefore, there was an expectation that the loans would result in some periodic benefit to the employees as the loans were retired. The principal retired for the period was considered to be a reasonable measure of the compensation expense.

In 1977, the IRS and DOL released final regulations that provided that the ESOP participants would receive an annual allocation as the shares were released from collateral. These regulations established two methods of collateral release: the principal-and-interest method and the principal-only method. In the first case, shares are released from collateral and allocated to participants on the basis of the ratio of the current year's payment of principal and interest to the total of the current year's payments plus all future year's payments of principal and interest. The principal-only method is simply the ratio of the current year's principal payment to the total original principal of the loan. The principal-only method is limited by three specific requirements of the regulations. The major limit is to ESOP loans that at all times have cumulative principal payments of no less than a normal 10-year amortization loan.

For many years, the SOP interpretation measuring compensation expense by the principal payment for the period did not come into any serious question. Most ESOP loans had a fairly normal amortization schedule. However, the 1984 and 1986 tax acts created some valuable incentives for ESOP loans. These triggered a great deal of creativity in lending to ESOPs, resulting in long-term interest-only loans or variable principal payment loans. At this point, the measurement of compensation expense by the amount of principal was deemed to be no longer a valid reflection of the ESOP.

The EITF dealt with this issue for a large part of calendar year 1989. In September of that year, a conclusion was issued in the form of EITF Issue No. 89-8, "Non-level Payments of Employee Stock

Ownership Plan Debt." Surprisingly, in response to a prompt, persuasive, and negative public uproar, this position was withdrawn in October, and a new position was published in December. This new position is still contained in Issue No. 89-8, but it has a new title, "Expense Recognition for Employee Stock Ownership Plans." The title was changed to make sure that practitioners would realize that it applies in all cases, not only those that anticipate or experience nonlevel debt service structures.

The 1989 approach to measuring expense provides that the total annual expense of any ESOP is measured under the following formula:

$$\frac{\text{Shares Allocated for the Period}}{\text{Total Shares Purchased}} \times \text{Original Principal} + \text{Interest Expense} - \text{Dividends}$$

If the plan uses the principal-only method for releasing shares from collateral, this new formula will result in the same compensation expense as the old SOP interpretation. However, in the case of a principal-and-interest amortization schedule, this could result in a dramatically different number. For example, assume that the loan has equal annual payments of principal and interest of $260,000. The original principal amount is $2 million. In the initial year of the loan, the interest paid is $200,000 and the principal paid is $60,000. Under the former interpretation of the SOP, the compensation expense would have been $60,000, the amount of principal paid on the loan for the year. Under the EITF consensus, the compensation expense would be approximately $133,000. This is one-fifteenth the amount of the original principal, as one-fifteenth of the shares would be released during this period.

In issuing this opinion, the EITF acknowledged that this was another major departure from the ESOP accounting rules that had previously applied. In this case, instead of transactional relief, a corridor of reasonableness was defined. If the plan sponsor's method of measuring expense, at all times, yields an expense that is at least equal to 80% of the cumulative expense calculated under EITF Issue 89-8 (before deduction of dividends), the plan sponsor's method will be considered acceptable. Of course, the sponsor's method must be based on some reasonable interpretation of SOP 76-3. In our example, if the plan sponsor had used the old SOP interpretation, the total expense would have been $260,000. The EITF expense was

$333,000. Since $260,000 is less than 80% of $333,000, a total expense of $267,000 (80% of $333,000) would be required for the first year, assuming the loan and method existed before December 14, 1989.

In this example, it has been assumed that all of the debt service has been satisfied through employer contributions to the plan, not dividends. However, the EITF did provide that any expense resulting by this formula must be reduced to the extent that it is paid from dividends. It did not mention, however, how that reduction would take place. Is compensation expense first reduced, then interest? Is it proportional? Does it follow how the cash was actually applied? Does it follow the terms of the plan? In our example above, if the stock carried an 8% dividend rate and the dividend was used entirely to service the debt, the total expense would be reduced by $160,000. If applied fully against compensation expense, the result would be a $27,000 credit in compensation expense for the current year. Alternatively, compensation could be reduced to $0 (zero) with the remaining $27,000 used to reduce the interest expense. Other approaches might be equally "reasonable." Given the accounting community's desire for consistency and uniformity, the issue needed to be addressed to eliminate any undesirable diversity in practice.

This was only one of the many unanswered questions that remained after the publication of this EITF consensus. Other questions that practitioners and plan sponsors raised included:

- How is the number of shares released for the period determined?
- What if the plan year varies from the plan sponsor's reporting year?
- Are we to measure shares released on the basis of the date the principal is paid and collateral is theoretically released, or the date that the participant accounting is performed and the shares are actually allocated to the accounts of the participants?
- What expense is recognized if the current contribution includes cash to meet future debt service obligations?

Income Statement Presentation Under SOP 93-6

SOP 93-6 eliminates the previous categorization of ESOPs into those using the principal-only method and those using the principal-plus-interest method of ESOP loan repayment. Instead, all new ESOPs or new stock acquisitions by former ESOPs will be included in a single accounting model. It also answers many of the unanswered questions noted earlier.

Under the revised proposal, compensation cost will be based on the average fair market value of the shares released or committed to be released with respect to any payments made on the ESOP debt for that year. This amount would be reduced for the shares released attributable to any dividends paid on allocated, but not unallocated, shares. This new method will have a dramatic impact when stock values go up or down significantly. Where share value increases rapidly, for example, compensation costs will be much higher than before. Average value for the year is used as the stock is assumed to have been earned throughout the year.

For example, the employer sponsors a 401(k) plan with a match. The match for the current plan year is $100,000. That match is going to be satisfied with the fair market value of employer securities released by the current year's contribution to the plan. Assume that the contribution required to release $100,000 of securities is only $80,000 (e.g., the company is using the principal-only method of collateral release, and the shares have increased in value by 25%).

Under the new model, the journal entries would be:

Compensation Cost	$100,000	
Accrued Matching Contribution		$100,000

· To record the accrual of the matching contribution:

Accrued Matching Contribution	$100,000	
ESOP Debt	$ 80,000	
Cash		$ 80,000
Unearned ESOP Shares Account		$ 80,000
Paid-in-Capital		$ 20,000

To record the payment of the match and the elimination of the ESOP debt and contra account, the increase in the market value of the stock is added to paid-in-capital. Note that if it was known that the matching contribution was to be satisfied through a contribution to the ESOP and associated release of shares, the accrued matching contribution would not be recorded.

This fair market value approach will be applied to all new ESOPs and all new acquisitions of shares by existing ESOPs but not to refinancings of old acquisitions, unless the sponsor has elected to apply this standard.

To deal with the problem that this fair market value model presents for the nontraded marketplace, SOP 93-6 does allow for management to estimate the value of the shares at year-end and then direct the auditor to test that value using such evidence as an independent determination of value that is no more than 12 months out of date from the statement date.

Earnings per Share: Reporting Considerations Through 1992

In the calculation of earnings per share, the same pattern reappears. Here, again, the 1976 SOP was based on a pattern of events that was much simpler than the structure of ESOPs that were being presented to the accounting community some years later. In drafting the original 1976 SOP, the AcSEC seemed to contemplate a world of only common stock ESOPs. If the committee even anticipated a preferred stock ESOP, it was probably not considered to be any different from the situation that would have been presented in those days if a nonleveraged stock bonus plan had invested in preferred stock. There was a simple answer given: paragraph 11 of SOP 76-3 provides simply that all shares of stock held by the ESOP, whether allocated or not, are to be treated as outstanding for purposes of calculating the plan sponsor's earnings per share.

However, the ESOP practices that evolved during the late 1980s included very specific types of convertible preferred stocks. These stocks have conversion features and floor price options that were specifically designed to meet the stringent standards of the Internal Revenue Code (the "Code") to enable the plan sponsor to deduct from taxable income the dividends paid on such shares that were used to service the ESOP's acquisition debt.

During 1989, there was a great deal of discussion on this issue within the accounting community. The issue was discussed by the EITF at many meetings throughout the summer and fall of the year. Final resolution came at the December 14, 1989, meeting of the EITF, where the EITF released Issue No. 89-12, "Earnings-per-Shares Issues Related to Convertible Preferred Stock Issued to an Employee Stock Ownership Plan." This consensus addresses four points:

1. Convertible preferred shares issued to an ESOP will not be considered to be common stock equivalents unless the yield at the date of issuance is less than $66^2/_3\%$ of the corporate Aa bond rate. This yield test is found in SFAS No. 85, "Yield Test for Determining Whether a Convertible Security is a Common Stock Equivalent." From the SEC's perspective, this may not be the only test. Reread the comments above regarding the plan sponsor's ability to retain the stock in permanent equity.

2. The difference between the preferred stock dividend and the common stock dividend is a "nondiscretionary adjustment," as described in paragraph 51 of APB Opinion No. 15, "Earnings per Share." This is because if the shares are assumed to have been converted, only the common dividends would have been available for debt service. If all of the dividends had actually been used for debt service, an additional contribution by the employer would have been required to cover the difference between the higher preferred stock dividend and the lower common stock dividend. (Note: in reaching this conclusion, the EITF did not concern itself with whether or not any additional contribution could have been made to the plan without violating the Code Section 415 limits and potentially disqualifying the plan. This point was raised by commentators, but the EITF apparently did not believe that the tax considerations were material to the accounting issue.)

3. In certain preferred stock ESOPs, the preferred stock has a guaranteed floor price that exceeds the current market value of the common stock into which the preferred can be converted. The EITF concluded that paragraph 63 of APB Opinion 15 applies in such a situation. In this case, earnings per share calculated under the if-converted method should include the number of shares that are assumed to be issued on the basis of the stated conversion rate for the unallocated shares, plus the number of shares that would be equivalent to the redemption value, but not less than the stated conversion rate, for allocated shares of convertible preferred stock. This rule applies only to the shares allocated as of the reporting date. (This raises an issue: Because earnings per share are reported quarterly, will this require quarterly allocations for publicly traded ESOPs?)

4. As a modification of the third item above, the EITF further decided that if the plan sponsor is either required, or has the ability and has expressed the intent, to satisfy the guaranteed floor value feature in cash, the stated conversion rate should be used for all shares and no additional issuance of shares related to the guarantee feature will be assumed.

Note: With respect to items 3 and 4 above, in the event that the assumed conversion is anti-dilutive, no conversion is to be assumed. When this consensus was achieved, the SEC observer to the EITF announced that the SEC would be enforcing this position retroactively. That is, any SEC companies would be required to apply this position retroactively to earnings-per-share calculations for all filings after the meeting date, December 14, 1989. This includes the restatement of prior EPS calculations that are contained in these filings.

SOP 93-6 Impact on the Measurement of Earnings per Share

For nonleveraged ESOPs, all shares are now considered outstanding, whether common or convertible preferred. For leveraged ESOPs, only the shares allocated, released, or committed to be released are considered outstanding. In all cases, convertible preferred stock is to be considered a common stock equivalent. This change will reduce the number of shares considered outstanding until an ESOP loan is fully amortized.

Statements of Cash Flows

The third financial statement is the statement of cash flow. The existence of an ESOP does not change the content or the presentation of this financial statement. Also, the shift from SOP 76-3 to SOP 93-6 has not had a material impact on this statement.

However, if the amount is material, there may be one or more line items included on this statement relative to the ESOP. If shares are contributed to the plan, they will be reflected as a non-cash expenditure. If the compensation cost reported varies from the cash contribution made to the plan, there may be a difference.

These results are not unexpected, but the impact of these concepts on loan covenants is frequently overlooked.

Footnote Disclosures

A general consensus of accounting authority recommends disclosure of the following information:

- A plan description, including the purpose, qualified status, contribution formula, and a description of the employer's securities held by the plan. Further, the number of allocated, released, committed to be released, and unallocated shares should be disclosed.
- An ESOP loan description, including the terms, interest rate, and payment commitments.
- A disclosure of the repurchase commitment on nontraded, distributed shares. To the extent that shares have been put to the employer before the end of the fiscal year, the liability would have to be booked, not just footnoted.

There is no requirement to record the projected repurchase obligation, even if the amount is significant. Under SOP 93-6, the repurchase obligation is still not required to be recorded on the financial statements. Nor is any actuarial projection to be required for footnote disclosure. Instead, the footnote disclosure will require that the current value of any allocated shares be disclosed. For this purpose, "current value" means as of the most recent valuation date.

Because of the new method of expense recognition required by EITF 89-8 and the related corridor for other allowable methods, the SEC has required that SEC registrants disclose their method of recognizing expense and the specific impact of the ESOP on their financial statements. In addition, they are asking for disclosure of the amount of any dividends that are used to service ESOP debt.

Even with the issuance of SOP 93-6, a diversity in accounting practices will still exist, since prior ESOP transactions will be allowed to retain their prior accounting. Therefore, disclosures will be required regarding which method of accounting is being used for any ESOP transactions included within the financials.

The footnote disclosures required by SOP 93-6 are not subject to the grandfather rule. The same disclosures are required whether the shares were acquired before or after the effective date of the standard.

Special Issues

ESOP Dividends

The 1984 and 1986 revisions to the Code provided for tax-deductible dividends to the extent such dividends are paid into an ESOP and distributed to participants or used to amortize an ESOP loan. That change, combined with the favorable accounting resulting from the use of dividends for debt service, contributed to the establishment of many plans that projected that a significant portion of securities acquisition debt would be retired with dividends.

Reporting the Dividend

Initially, for financial statement reporting purposes, these dividends were still dividends chargeable to retained earnings, not compensation expense. The exception was for dividends on unallocated shares arising from an excess contribution or a prepayment of debt. In such cases, the transaction is accounted for under the treasury stock method, and these dividends are treated as compensation expense (see EITF Issue 86-27).

This is an area that changed dramatically under SOP 93-6. The rules are reflected in the most complicated section of the standard. Effectively, when ESOP dividends can be used to satisfy an obligation that otherwise would have had to have been satisfied by an employer contribution, the dividends will affect the income statement presentation of the plan sponsor.

The clearest argument can be made for dividends paid on unallocated shares. Under the terms of the plan, these dividends can be applied by the trustee to make debt payments on the securities acquisition debt; to be distributed to plan participants; or to be retained in the trust (although allocated to the accounts of plan participants) for other purposes, including building up the value of participants' accounts. In all cases, these dividends are treated as having lost their character as dividends. This is simply because the value of those dividends does not remain attached to the securities on which they were paid. Instead, the plan sponsor, through plan design or directions to the trustee, is able to use them to satisfy other objectives or benefit other participants within the plan. The effect of this argument is that dividends paid on unallocated shares will generally result in compensation cost.

Dividends paid on allocated shares are treated differently. The value of the dividend must stay with the shares on which it was paid. This is true even where the plan sponsor chooses to use that dividend to service the securities acquisition debt. The tax rules require that where these dividends are used to satisfy the debt, shares must be returned to the participant's account that are worth at least as much as the dividends that were withdrawn from that account to service the debt (Code Section 404(k)).

In drafting the SOP, the AcSEC took the position that the requirement to replace allocated dividends used for debt service with stock of at least an equivalent value is a significant event that should be reported separately from the payment of the dividend. When existing ESOP shares are used to meet this obligation (referred to as the "dividend make-up"), the value of the shares on the date that they are released or committed to be released for this purpose should be used to report the satisfaction of the liability. If the plan sponsor contributes additional shares to the plan to meet this obligation, the contribution of those new shares would be reflected in compensation cost at their current value.

Dividends on released but unallocated shares are to be accounted for in the same manner as dividends on allocated shares.

Reporting the Tax Benefit of ESOP Dividends

A tax benefit may be realized on these payments. The amount of such benefit is not always obvious because of the potential impact of the alternative minimum tax. The tax benefit from these dividends was originally recorded as an adjustment to retained earnings (see EITF 86-4).

1. Under SFAS 109, the tax benefit of the ESOP dividend will be classified differently depending on whether it is applicable to allocated or unallocated shares. The tax benefit applicable to unallocated shares will follow how the dividend is classified. If dividends are charged to retained earnings, the tax benefit will be also. If dividends are charged, directly or indirectly, to compensation cost, the tax benefit will stay in the income statement. All of the tax benefits associated with dividends on allocated shares can be used to reduce the current income tax obligation. See paragraphs 33 and 34 and the related footnote. Note that, as

discussed above, under the new standard dividends on unallocated shares will not go to retained earnings. The general inference is that any tax benefit on these dividends would be covered by paragraph 33 of the SFAS.

2. The accounting for dividends described above was further expanded in EITF Issue 90-4, "Earnings-per-Share Treatment of Tax Benefits for Dividends on Stock Held by an Employee Stock Ownership Plan." This pronouncement addresses an omission of prior pronouncements: the EPS consequences. New EITF Consensus Opinion 92-3 clarifies that the benefit from common stock dividends on unallocated shares cannot be added back in calculating EPS.

   The first aspect of this consensus deals with whether any ESOP preferred stock dividends should be deducted from net income net of any applicable income tax benefit for purposes of computing primary earnings per share. At its March 8, 1990, meeting the EITF concluded that if the preferred stock is not a common stock equivalent, then the preferred dividends would be deducted net of tax from net income for purposes of calculating primary earnings per share.

   The second issue discussed was whether the tax benefits related to common dividends should be considered net income for purposes of computing earnings per share. No consensus was reached on this issue.

   The third and final issue discussed related to the disclosures required for these transactions. Here the EITF concluded that the amount and treatment, in the EPS computation, of the tax benefit related to any dividend paid to an ESOP must be disclosed, if material.

ESOPs in Leveraged Buyouts

Accounting for ESOP transactions becomes particularly complicated when the ESOP is a party to a leveraged buyout of an entity. In these situations, the ESOP accounting complexities are added to the purchase accounting issues presented by any business combination. This discussion is outside the scope of this chapter. It is critical to recognize that the business combination rules basically are applied first to the reporting, and the impact of the ESOP as a provider of some of the financing is only then integrated into the reporting. Where preferred shares are used or where shares are transferred over a period of time, special rules may apply.

Defined Benefit Reversions

The Tax Reform Act of 1986 made it attractive to transfer excess assets from a defined benefit plan to fund an ESOP. When transferred, this excess did not have to be allocated to the benefit of plan participants within a single year. Instead, the benefit might be allocable in as many as eight separate plan years. The concept of an excess contribution to a defined contribution plan, like an ESOP, where the contribution was not immediately allocated, was foreign to the accounting community. Therefore, the EITF was called upon to draft a position on this fact pattern. This was done in EITF Issue No. 86-27.

For the most part, this consensus follows the same theory as the 76-3 SOP on leveraged ESOPs. The unallocated shares are placed in a suspense account that resides in the equity section of the balance sheet. As shares are released from suspense and allocated to participants, the related compensation expense is to be recorded. However, in the treatment of dividends and the measurement of the amount of the compensation expense, this consensus varies dramatically from the SOP. Compensation expense is measured by the fair market value of the shares released. If distributed to participants, dividends paid on unallocated shares would be deductible as compensation expense, not charged to retained earnings like other dividends. Further, if dividends on unallocated stock were used to prepay debt, they would also be deductible as compensation. Finally, this consensus also varied from the SOP in the calculation of earnings per share. As you recall under the SOP, all shares, allocated and unallocated, are considered to be outstanding in determining EPS. Under EITF 86-27, only the allocated shares are considered outstanding.

In subsequent meetings, the EITF specifically limited the application of these concepts to only the case of the transfer of a defined benefit plan excess to an ESOP. Therefore, employers may not seek to make comparison to other ESOP applications for a similar accounting theory.

The tax advantage that created this planning technique expired on December 31, 1988. Because of this, the application of this is limited to those companies that effected such transfers within the permitted time frame. Although this position is more current than that taken in SOP 76-3, it is not clear how fully the EITF understood ESOPs at the time it made this decision. It is probably not realistic to anticipate that any future pronouncements on ESOP accounting will follow the trends of this position, any more than they might follow the trend of SOP 76-3.

If such a transaction took place today, the terms of the EITF Consensus Opinion would have to be modified to reflect SOP 93-6.

S Corporations

Since the law was changed in 1998 to permit S corporations to have an ESOP as a shareholder, many ESOP sponsors have elected S corporation status. An S corporation does not pay income taxes directly. Rather, taxable income is passed through to shareholders who then pay tax or not based upon their own tax situation. Under current law, an ESOP is exempt from tax on income passed through from an S corporation as long as a variety of technical requirements are satisfied.

The S election does not change the format of the financial statements, nor does it change the general rules described above for the accounting of ESOP transactions. However, there are some unique financial reporting consequences to an S election that need to be considered:

1. When a company changes to S corporation status, deferred taxes do not have to be recognized for any temporary book/tax differences occurring after the date of the change in tax status, except in the case of post-1986 S corporation elections discussed below. When a company converts from C corporation status to S corporation status, it must retain an existing deferred tax liability to the extent it would be subject to built-in gains tax. The deferred tax liability will continue to be remeasured at each balance sheet date until the end of the 10-year period. Any other deferred tax amounts are eliminated as of the date of change from C to S status.

2. Under the Revenue Act of 1987, a company with LIFO inventories electing S corporation status after December 17, 1987 will include its LIFO reserve in its last return filed as a C corporation. The tax is payable in equal amounts over four years, with

the first payment due by the due date (not including extensions) of the last return filed as a C corporation. The total liability should be accrued and charged to income tax expense applicable to income from continuing operations at the date of change. When a company is subject to the LIFO recapture requirement, the LIFO recapture represents a new LIFO base for income tax purposes. However, for financial statement purposes the LIFO recapture requirement does not affect the LIFO base. Accordingly, it will be necessary for those affected companies to maintain LIFO cost records separately for income tax and financial statement purposes.

3. Similar rules to the LIFO recapture apply to financial institutions with respect to bad debt reserves. The built-in gains rules are also more complicated for financial institutions.

4. Under current authority, S corporations are only permitted to use distributions on unallocated shares for debt service, and there is no tax benefit associated with such dividends. Thus, the financial reporting consequences for debt payments from S corporation distributions are easier to understand and to apply. Fundamentally, such distributions run through compensation cost when it is charged for the average fair value of the shares released attributable to those S corporation distributions.

5. Because other plan terms may also change with the election of S status, the footnote disclosures for the ESOP may change.

Practical Applications

As tables 7-1 and 7-2 illustrate, the impact of a leveraged ESOP on a company's balance sheet is dramatic. Financial ratios, like debt to equity, are substantially affected. This case was fairly minor, as it anticipated that the capital would stay in the company. When the capital is leaving the company to repurchase the stock of a retiring shareholder, circumstances become even more exotic. In this case, it is not at all unusual to see a negative equity section.

In many cases the "adverse" consequences of the accounting treatment can be minimized through a well-planned transaction. In some cases, the accounting rules cannot be managed. For example, until the users of statements become more sophisticated, the ESOP accounting rules simply will not allow for a highly leveraged ESOP

Accounting for Employee Stock Ownership Plan Transactions

TABLE 7-1. Traditional Leveraged ESOP.

Balance Sheet: Pre-ESOP

		Accounts Payable	$ 30,000
		Bank Debt	10,000
		Total Liabilities	$ 40,000
		Stockholders' Equity	70,000
Total Assets	$110,000	Total Liability and Stockholders' Equity	$110,000

Balance Sheet: Post-ESOP

		Accounts Payable	$ 30,000
		Bank Debt	10,000
		ESOP Debt	1,000
		Total Liabilities	$ 41,000
		Stockholders' Equity	$ 71,000
		ESOP Contra Account	(1,000)
		Total Stockholders' Equity	$ 70,000
Total Assets	$111,000	Total Liability and Stockholders' Equity	$111,000

Balance Sheet: Post-ESOP, Year 2
No changes except the payment of principal on ESOP note. Assume no profit or loss before contribution of principal (compensation expense) and interest. The principal-only method of collateral release is used. Therefore, compensation expense equals principal payment.

		Accounts Payable	$ 30,000
		Bank Debt	10,000
		ESOP Debt	900
		Total Liabilities	$ 40,900
		Stockholders' Equity	$ 71,000
		ESOP Contra Account	(900)
		Current Year's Loss	(200)
		Total Stockholders' Equity	$ 69,900
Total Assets	$110,800	Total Liability and Stockholders' Equity	$110,800

TABLE 7-2. *Two-Step ESOP Loan.*

Balance Sheet: Pre-ESOP

		Accounts Payable	$ 30,000
		Bank Debt	10,000
		Total Liabilities	$ 40,000
		Stockholders' Equity	70,000
Total Assets	$110,000	Total Liability and Stockholders' Equity	$110,000

Balance Sheet: Post-ESOP

		Accounts Payable	$ 30,000
		Bank Debt	11,000
		Total Liabilities	$ 41,000
		Stockholders' Equity	$ 71,000
		ESOP Receivable	(1,000)
		Total Stockholders' Equity	$ 70,000
Total Assets	$110,000	Total Liability and Stockholders' Equity	$111,000

that is used to retire a former owner in an enterprise whose ability to do business is a current function of its equity section, for example, an enterprise subject to bonding or a financial institution. In all cases, the accounting needs to be discussed at the beginning of the transaction, not after closing.

Alternative options are available for companies that could not tolerate the accounting consequences of recording the ESOP debt on the balance sheet and the offsetting, negative impact on the equity section. Unfortunately, these alternatives require the loss of some ESOP advantages in exchange for the less objectionable accounting treatment.

Nonleveraged ESOP

Under this approach, the ESOP does not use debt financing to purchase the shares. Instead, an annual cash contribution is made to the plan, which it uses to purchase shares or the plan sponsor simply contributes shares to the plan. Since there is no ESOP debt in this case, there is no need to record the debt or the offsetting contra-equity entry. However, this transaction means that there is not a single purchase of stock that qualifies for all the leveraged ESOP incentives. Instead, there will be a series of purchases that may eventually qualify for certain ESOP incentives.

The primary cash flow advantage of an ESOP can be simulated with this approach. This is the deductible principal. Assume a company needed $1 million in additional capital. It could borrow the funds from a lender under a typical commercial loan. As annual principal payments are required, the company could contribute to the ESOP shares with a value equal to that year's principal payment. Assuming that the contribution was within the limitations of Section 404(a)(3) of the Code, the company would get a tax deduction for a noncash expense, the contribution of stock. Thus its cash flow picture would be exactly the same as if the ESOP had borrowed the $1 million and it had made a plan contribution sufficient to amortize the debt. (However, a leveraged ESOP may offer more tax incentives, as discussed in the first chapter of this book.)

Partially Leveraged ESOP

In some cases, plan sponsors have some flexibility in taking on ESOP financing, but they cannot take the entire piece in one year. In these transactions, a combination of the nonleveraged plan and a smaller leveraged plan can be used. For example, rather than a single purchase of 30% of the company, three separate sales of 10% each are arranged over a period of years. The seller cannot obtain the tax-deferred sale benefit on the first two sales, but the trade-off is that the transaction can be handled without the major negative entry into the equity section and the disruption of the plan sponsor's bonding capacity or other business operations that are based on the equity section.

Conclusion

The advantages of ESOPs can be maximized and the disadvantages minimized with proper planning. A clear picture of what the accounting effects of an ESOP will be should be considered at the earliest possible stage of planning for an ESOP.

The financial reporting for ESOP transactions has been and continues to be in a state of change. As such, ESOP sponsors and corporations contemplating the implementation of an ESOP need to be sensitive to this.

Chapter 8

The Feasibility Study for the Employee-Led Buyout

Deborah Groban Olson

Purchasing a company is a complex undertaking for any buyer.[1] For employees buying on a leveraged[2] basis, the complexity is increased both by the added debt and by changes in company leadership and investment structure that affect everyone who deals with the company. Anyone considering such a purchase must perform a thorough investigation of the company as it exists and forecast the effect of the changes such a proposed transaction is likely to create. This chapter will address the feasibility study conducted in association with a leveraged buyout (LBO) of a company or part of a company in which the employees, through an employee stock ownership plan (ESOP), constitute the buyer and are leading the transaction.

Special Issues in the Transition to Employee Ownership

Labor and Employee Benefit Issues, Including Concessions

Often, employee ownership is proposed to save a troubled company. Performing a prefeasibility study will generally determine whether the company is too troubled for further consideration and whether there is a willing seller at a reasonable price. Once past that hurdle, the question often arises whether employees will give up some portion of fixed wages and/or benefits and instead receive stock ownership and profit or gain sharing. Careful cost-benefit analysis of the options is required. Key questions for employees to answer before agreeing on any particular concession level are:

- What is the economic present value of the concessions, and how does it compare with the investments being made by other parties to the transaction? What is the value of the stock being offered to the employees? Do the employees have any more favorable alternative?
- Does the financial analysis used in the feasibility study or business plan cover a long enough time frame to show how employees are likely to fare upon retirement?
- Has the company planned to have the cash available for repurchasing the stock from employees upon their retirement?
- Pension obligations, environmental matters, and retiree health insurance liability are all factors that bear close attention from anyone performing a feasibility study. Employees reviewing such a study should pay close attention to proposed solutions to company financial problems that may affect their retirement benefits.
- Unionized employees should contact their international union research department or resources such as the Ohio Employee Ownership Center (OEOC) for more information on negotiating employee ownership.

Continuity and Transition Issues: Management, Customers, Markets

Any company going through an ownership change has a series of transition issues to handle. It is most important to have a positive public relations strategy explaining the buyout effort. Many people mistakenly think that an employee buyout is a last-ditch effort to save a failing company. However, employee ownership is often born of employee interest in getting a piece of the action in a good company or because the owners wish to retire. It is important to have a presentation on this subject ready for customers and suppliers, particularly if they may be contacted as part of a feasibility study.

Management and all employees may well be nervous about job security during a feasibility study. If a company is overstaffed or poorly managed, there may be a need to change some of the personnel in an employee buyout. These decisions should be made with care, caution, and objectivity. Every effort should be made to keep personal allegiances and politics out of such decisions by using assistance from outside consultants. The buyout committee should work to instill such values in its membership.

Transition from Subsidiary to Stand-Alone Company

It is not extremely difficult to replace many central corporate functions such as accounting, information systems, personnel, employee benefits administration, or the legal department—services that can be readily purchased from outside vendors. Often these can be handled at a savings over the corporate charge. The most difficult change is usually in marketing and distribution, and in some cases in engineering or product development. If these are critical issues for the business, take special care that your feasibility study includes industry expertise in evaluating these problems and proposing solutions.

What Is a Feasibility Study?

A feasibility study attempts to provide an accurate picture of the company as it currently exists and to project what it will look like over the next three to five years, based on proposed changes in ownership, financing, markets, product, costs of labor and raw materials, technology, the economy, and so on. A feasibility study attempts to assess the future viability of the target company and the ability of that company to support a proposed buyout transaction. In undertaking this effort, the feasibility study strives to predict the future, based on knowledge of the past and the application of assumptions about the future. The study usually includes a comparison of the target business with other competitors or similar businesses to see how it compares on a variety of business and financial criteria. The study is only as good as the past information, the validity of the future assumptions, and the care and detail with which the financial model(s) of the company are constructed.

Anyone seeking to borrow money to buy a company will have to provide all the lenders with a feasibility study and a business plan. The study will have to show how the buyers plan to make enough money in the purchased business, over the term of the loan, to repay the loan out of cash flow and retain enough money to maintain and reinvest appropriately in the business so it will grow or at least retain its value.

The Time Frame Covered

As a buyer or part of a buyer group, it is important to understand that the lenders are primarily interested in feasibility studies and business plans that study the term of their loan(s). A typical ESOP term loan financed with senior bank debt usually runs for five to seven years. A buyer, particularly a group of young employees, may be concerned with a much longer time frame. If they are planning to own the company through an ESOP and obtain their ESOP benefit at retirement, the buyers may want a feasibility study to look at a longer-term perspective than the one of most interest to the lenders. It is possible to have the same consultant provide a study covering the term of interest to the lenders, and also to create additional scenarios showing the buyers what the farther future is likely to look like. However, most consultants who provide feasibility studies are very wary of the veracity of any assumptions beyond three years.

Obtaining and Relying on Company Data

One key indicator of the likelihood for a successful transaction is the willingness of the seller to provide the financial data needed to perform a feasibility study. Often a seller will want the prospective buyer or its consultants to sign a "confidentiality agreement."[3] If financial data are not forthcoming after the buyer has offered to sign a confidentiality agreement, it is likely that the seller is not seriously interested in selling to the buyer group. Unless the buyer has some other leverage over the seller, this may be the time to kill the deal.

Large companies (and many smaller ones) are likely to have audited financial statements. In that case the financial information is usually provided in a standard format and may be reliable. However, it is crucial to read the cover letter accompanying any financial statements prepared by an outside accountant to determine what the financial statements actually are and how much investigation the outside accountant did to verify the numbers. There are significant differences between "audited" financial statements, where the accountant actually tests the underlying data, and various "compilations" provided by accountants, which are simply standard arrangements of information as provided by management, without any testing. The cover letter may also show deviations from standard accounting procedures and may include an accountant's opinion about the viability of the business.

Many companies do not have audited financial statements. This does not mean they are financially weak. It may simply mean that they have never had a need to go to the expense and trouble to get audited financial statements. However, if you are going to borrow significant funds to purchase a company, the lender will require audited financial statements in the future.

In either event, whether audited or unaudited, you cannot simply rely on the company's data when you buy the company. You must perform your own due diligence to determine whether the information given you is accurate. If it is not, you need to figure out a way to obtain accurate data. For the purposes of a prefeasibility study, you may assume that the company's data are correct. Then you will study whether, assuming that information is correct, the company is worth buying. You will probably need a qualified professional—such as an investment banker, an appraiser, or an accountant—with experience in reviewing company financial data to help you determine what the company's data really means.

Finding Resources and Hiring Consultants

Prefeasibility Study Versus Full Feasibility Study

Often, a buyer will do a preliminary feasibility study (a prefeasibility study, often referred to as a "quick and dirty" study) to determine if it makes sense to invest the time, effort, and money needed to complete a full feasibility study to weed out obvious deal killers. A prefeasibility study uses readily available sources of information.

There is not a bright line between prefeasibility and full feasibility studies. Both may include much of the information provided in a business plan for the proposed business. The more information you can get in a prefeasibility study the better, so long as you get the results in enough time to take action. The items listed below as belonging in a prefeasibility study are basically those that the State of Michigan (until 1999) got consultants to provide for $10,000 in 21 days using funding from the Job Training Partnership Act (JTPA) and the Economic Dislocation and Worker Adjustment Assistance Act (EDWAA). Most consultants believed they performed much more than $10,000 worth of work to provide such information. Many of the details included therein are normally thought to be part of a full feasibility study

Resources

In August 1998, federal funding to states to assist dislocated workers began to be provided under the Workforce Investment Act (WIA) instead of the JTPA. There is considerable regional and state control over the administration of the WIA funds. Dislocated worker funds are used for a variety of programs, so the amount, if any, earmarked for feasibility studies varies, and the process to access the funds varies state-by-state. However, an interested citizen should be able to locate the appropriate agency by contacting the governor's office, state economic development agency or state office of workforce development. At least a few prefeasibility studies in 2003 and 2004 received WIA funding approval for $15,000 for a period of 30 to 45 days.

Under the WIA, most states have funds they can make available (usually up to $25, 000) to pay for a prefeasibility study for a potential employee buyout in circumstances where a plant closing is likely. Often that means that a Workers Adjustment and Retraining Notification (WARN) notice has been given. Different states have different requirements for buyer groups to receive such funds. Some states have pre-approved consultants whom the state hires to do the study after the prospective buyer group has approached the state for assistance. Some states give the regional workforce development agency the responsibility for hiring consultants. Other organizations, such as labor unions, often require a prefeasibility study to determine whether more resources should be expended on the project. It may be possible to have a nonprofit organization or a university business school provide a prefeasibility study on a pro bono basis if other sources of funding are not available.

Government funding for feasibility studies in situations where no shutdown is threatened is very rarely available. However, employee buyout associations (discussed below) have been very creative in obtaining funds from a great variety of local sources, especially where the employees themselves have first contributed some funds.

In the case of owners of closely held companies selling to an ESOP, however, a feasibility study may not really be as complex as in a buyout of a failing company, a corporate division, or a large company. An interested seller may be willing to provide some resources for the employees to perform a study. This chapter focuses on the more complex transactions. A feasibility assessment in a business continuity situation would essentially be a comparable to the preparation of a business plan for a loan.

Another important resource that may be able to provide free or low-cost help for the manufacturing and technology assessment are the Manufacturing Extension Technology agencies funded by the National Institute of Standards and Technology (NIST) *(www.nist.gov)*. NIST is a nonregulatory federal agency within the U.S. Commerce Department's Technology Administration. It operates four cooperative programs, one of which is the Manufacturing Extension Partnership (MEP).

The MEP is a nationwide network of local centers offering technical and business assistance to smaller manufacturers. You can locate the center nearest to you on the Web at *www.mep.nist.gov/about-mep/center-info.html*. A map of the nation (including the several states) will appear, and you can either click on your state to locate your nearest center or go to a page listing all the MEP centers across the U.S. Alternatively, you can call 1-800-MEP-4MFG (1-800-637-4634), and your call will automatically be routed to your nearest center.

In Michigan, benchmarking assessments are carried out by the Michigan Manufacturing and Technology Center (MMTC), which has six offices across the state. For more information, visit *www.iti.org*. The MMTC is funded by the NIST Manufacturing Extension Program and the Michigan Economic Development Corporation. MMTC provides a free benchmarking assessment yearly, upon request, to certain types of Michigan manufacturing businesses. A benchmarking report compares a business to its competitors on a wide variety of manufacturing, technology, quality, sales, and purchasing factors. Such a study can help pinpoint a business' strengths and weaknesses. It can help the buyout committee and its consultants compare the current management's view of these issues against external objective criteria.

The Focus of a Prefeasibility Study: A Quick "Go" or "No Go"

A prefeasibility study looks at the major factors that may cause the prospective buyer to stop the process, such as:

- Is there a willing seller who will cooperate with the buyer by providing information?
- Will the seller sell for a reasonable price?
- Has some major business change occurred, such as the loss of a major customer or account; the loss of an important lease, copyright, patent, technology, piece of expensive or unique equipment, etc.; a change in product or technology by a competitor that has massively realigned the market; or any other event that substantially ends the previous market as it existed?
- Has some physical or legal disaster incapacitated the business?
- Can the buyer obtain reliable financial data (income statements, cash flow and balance sheet information) from the last three to five years on the operation to be purchased?
- Are there management, labor, or other personnel issues that will inhibit a smooth transition to employee ownership?
- Does the employee buyout group have the necessary leadership to carry out an employee buyout?

The Buyout Association

Creating an employee buyout association provides hourly and management employees a structure for running the buyout process, including making decisions about hiring consultants; directing the buyout; forming a vision of employee ownership and priorities for the group as they negotiate with consultants, lenders and the seller; and forming a vehicle to raise funds from among themselves and/or receive funds from other sources, such as government agencies, concerned local citizens, or businesses or foundations.

When a group of employees begins the buyout process, it needs a prefeasibility study and then possibly some consultants. Initially, the group may obtain the prefeasibility study through a nonprofit or state agency. However, if the prefeasibility study is positive for pursuing a buyout, the group will need a variety of consultants, including:

- An attorney to help create a temporary structure for the buyout group, set up the permanent corporate and ESOP structures, and negotiate the legal aspects of the purchase.

- An investment banker or financial advisor to analyze the company's competitive position in the market and its operation, develop a business plan, structure the financing for the buyout, negotiate the financial aspects of the purchase, and find additional resources, such as new managers.
- An independent valuation consultant to value the ESOP stock and perhaps to provide a physical appraisal.
- A participation consultant if there is a desire to create a participative employee-owned company.

It is important for the group to focus on its vision of employee ownership and participation early on in the consultant hiring phase. The views and experiences of the consultants, as well as the group's contractual relationships with them, will affect the outcome of the employee-owned company.

Generally, a prefeasibility study is undertaken on an hourly or fixed fee basis and not on a contingency basis. You do not want your consultant to give you a positive answer in order to get paid. You do want the consultant to give you the truth.

Some investment bankers will do a free prefeasibility study on a project that interests them if you agree to hire them to handle the buyout transaction if there is a feasible project. This arrangement presents risks of a conflict of interest, which risks are sometimes warranted if a quick study is needed and if the buyout group has sufficient faith that the consultant will say "no" if the deal is bad and that the consultant will spend enough time on the study if the deal is marginal.

If a prefeasibility study shows that there is no reason to assume a purchase is not warranted, then a full study may be undertaken. It is also true that in many cases, after a prefeasibility study, a full study is not pursued; rather, the parties begin negotiations for a sale and save the further investigation for the "due diligence"[4] period after a "letter of intent offer"[5] has been signed.

The full feasibility study phase can also be referred to as the deal-structuring phase. Once a prefeasibility study has been done that shows that there is no obvious reason why an employee buyout should not work, the next stage is to structure the outline and parameters of the proposed transaction, create a business plan, and seek financing. Sometimes this takes the form of a feasibility study. Sometimes an investment banker is hired to attempt to put together a deal for the buyer. Much of the work is the same. The differences lie in the basis and nature of payment for the financial consultant's work and the definition of the final product.

If a feasibility study is sought and paid for, the lead consultant is still seeking an answer to the question: Should the client want to buy the company? The final work product is likely to be a study report. Once the report is delivered, the buyout group still has to develop a business plan, arrange financing for the transaction, and take care of the other matters upon which financing is contingent, such as selecting a new CEO and so on.

If a financed deal is the agreed-upon final work product, the study is often simply the preliminary act in financing and concluding a transaction. Usually, the lead consultant is an investment banker. Most often, the lead consultant is paid a retainer and a contingent success fee based on the amount and type of financing arranged. As part of the work, the lead consultant will find the additional elements needed to make financing feasible.

If a buyout group chooses to hire an investment banker on a success-fee basis to conclude a transaction, the buyout group must be very careful about the contract it structures with the investment banker. Once a success-fee arrangement has been signed, the investment banker performs a huge amount of work to conclude a transaction. If the deal does not close, the investment bank may make little or nothing for its time. There is a heavy incentive for the investment banker to close the deal. If the buyout group has minimum requirements for its definition of an acceptable transaction, it must set them out in its initial contract with the lead consultant and investment banker so that any contingent compensation is based not only on closing a deal but also on ensuring that the deal has the features agreed upon by the buyout group and its consultants in the consultant's contract.

A valuation consultant is usually paid on an hourly basis or on a per-project basis. The valuation consultant should have both ESOP valuation experience and knowledge of the company's industry.

Generally the attorney is paid on an hourly basis, although some of the attorney's fees may be paid out of the closing fees. An experienced employee ownership attorney can help structure the buyout group to operate as a decision-making and fund-raising body during the buyout process, help the buyout group negotiate contracts with other consultants that meet the buyout group's objectives, and develop the necessary corporate, ESOP, and transaction documents.

Costs of a Feasibility Study or Deal Structuring

Costs vary considerably depending on the size and complexity of the transaction. A prefeasibility study should generally be completed in less than six weeks and cost no more than $15,000 to $25,000. Many buyers skip the formal full feasibility study and go straight from the prefeasibility study to the deal-structuring phase. This accounts for the wide price range in the phase I refer to as "the full feasibility study." The entire full feasibility study package outlined below could range in price from $40,000 to $200,000.

However, if an investment banker handles the business plan, asset appraisal, and initial ESOP stock valuation fees on a contingent fee basis, those items may be rolled into a financing fee that is based on a percentage (or sliding scale of percentages) of the amount of financing obtained. Similarly, lenders will charge origination fees based on a percentage of the amount lent. The total fees on a $35 million transaction might be as much as $1 million or more. These are generally rolled into the financed purchase price.

There are a number of sources of financing for the feasibility study. The main ones are as follows:

- Existing owners.
- Employees. It is often helpful in finding matching funds to request at least a small contribution as a sign of commitment from employees. Often this is in the form of dues for membership in an employee buyout association. An employee buyout association also gives hourly and management employees a structure for making decisions about the direction of the buyout and provides a vehicle to receive funds from other sources, such as government agencies.
- Technical assistance grants from state agencies, the Federal Mediation and Conciliation Service, the Economic Development Administration, etc.
- Local city or county economic development agencies.
- Local benefactors, perhaps located through the union or mayor's office.

- Foundations, churches, community fundraising efforts, and unions.
- Pro bono work by local business schools, firms and universities.
- Contingent fee arrangements with consultants if you move directly to the deal-structuring mode that includes a feasibility study.

Finding and Choosing Consultants

Finding appropriate people can be difficult, but there are several good starting points. You can ask:

- Nonprofit groups specializing in worker ownership, university business schools, union research and legal departments, and other employee ownership companies.
- State economic research offices that have contact with economists and business analysts or state departments that serve your industry (departments of commerce, transportation, forestry, energy, etc.).
- Unions, chambers of commerce, or industry trade associations whose members may have used business consultants.
- University MBA programs at which you can ask the dean whether students undertake business consulting projects.
- Department heads of university marketing, finance, and business departments who may know the faculty who do this kind of work.

The National Center for Employee Ownership (NCEO) maintains a referral service of professional consultant members for member companies and employees. The NCEO can also provide initial non-technical advice to members, including a discussion of available options. You should interview at least three different consultants. Once you have found one or more likely individuals or groups, there are several questions that you must ask.

What to Look for in Potential Financial Consultants

- Have they done feasibility studies for employee buyouts or subsidiary divestitures?
- Have they done any market studies?
- Have they done financial modeling or prepared business plans?
- Have they had other business clients?
- Do they have extensive business/finance experience?
- Will they give you a list of clients for references?
- Can they get the study done within six to eight weeks (depending on your time pressures)?
- Are they willing to give opinions (with caveats) about issues for which all the data they would like are not available?

What to Look for in Valuation Consultants

- They must be independent of the seller and the company, meaning they have not done other work for either of those parties.
- They should work for the buyout association or the to-be-formed ESOP committee or its trustees.
- They should be familiar with the law, Department of Labor regulations, and cases defining "adequate consideration" and "fair market value."
- They should have experience in valuing stock for ESOP purposes (perhaps in your industry) and should be able to provide you with references.

What to Look for in ESOP Attorneys

- How many ESOPs have they worked on?
- Can they give you ESOP client references?
- Do you and the attorney have compatible views on employee ownership and participation?
- Do they have experience in structuring employee buyout associations and contracts between such associations and other consultants?

The Questions to Be Answered in a Prefeasibility Study

Your prefeasibility study should address the following issues:

Organizational Matters

Answers to the following questions will help you determine whether you have a group of employees who can carry out a buyout.

- Do you have leadership from the management side that can lead the management group during the buyout process and either is a potential CEO or can help you locate one?
- Have you created an employee buyout organization to assist with the prefeasibility study, to make decisions about the steps to be taken in the buyout effort, and to raise money to take action?
- Have you located resources to help you understand and carry out the employee buyout process? These may include a state or nonprofit agency, and/or legal or financial professionals experienced with employee buyouts.
- Do you have cooperation and leadership from the union, if there is one?
- Can your labor and management leaders cooperate on a major project?
- Do you have a willing seller?

What Is a Willing Seller?

This is a more difficult matter to determine than you would think. There is a saying that "everything is for sale for the right price." However, an individual private owner has no obligation to sell anything to anyone. A public company, or the board of directors of a privately held company with more than one stockholder, does have an obligation to consider bona fide purchase offers. A bona fide purchase offer is an offer for a price reasonably within market value that has a source of financing. Therefore, if the employee buyout group needs cooperation from the seller to get information in order to obtain financing, the seller can prevent the group from making a bona fide offer. In its simplest form, a hostile leveraged employee buyout purchase is a non-starter. An employee buyout from a willing seller is difficult enough.

The more difficult case is the seller who appears to be a willing seller but in fact has a buyer other than the employees that he or she favors, or who is unwilling to sell the company at an objective "fair market value." These issues should be addressed as quickly as possible.

If the seller has a favored buyer, try to find out as much as you can about that buyer, and see if you can make a deal to join up with the favored buyer. If not, assess your ability to timely develop a competitive bid. In such a situation you may wish to develop a backup bid in case the favored buyer's deal falls through. In that case you will still need your prefeasibility study.

If the seller is a closely held company, run by an individual, the buyout group should ask the individual what he or she wants for the business before starting on a feasibility study, and ask for the basis for the asking price. Early in the buyout process, as you are seeking valuation or financial professionals, you should ask whether the seller's initial price is in a reasonable ballpark. If it is not, you need to either develop a quick strategy for coming up with a ballpark number to discuss with the prospective seller or make a quick assessment of the items included in the asking price. If there is a great discrepancy between the asking price and your ballpark, you may have an unwilling seller. You may not get an asking price upon request. Rather, you may be asked to make an offer. This might indicate more openness from the seller. However, if you do not have access to necessary information, you cannot make an informed offer. A seller who is unwilling to disclose the financial, manufacturing, environmental, real estate, or other information you request from the company, upon your agreement (or that of your consultants) to provide a confidentiality agreement, is not a willing seller.

Market and Comparison Data

The following steps will help you determine whether the company is in a viable market.

- Obtain an overview of the industry and competition, including a forecast of demand and an assessment of market stability. Much of the information you need to compare your company to its competitors is available in published analyses, which you can find in a public or business school library, online, or from industry experts. Prime sources of data on your industry are available in libraries (such as public business libraries, university libraries, or major bank libraries), from your company, or from the following sources:

— Standard & Poor's Industry Surveys.

— Value Line Investment Survey.

— The Department of Commerce's U.S. Industrial Outlook (annual).

— Moody's Industrial Manual for your corporation or other companies in your industry (annual).

— Walker's Manual of Western Corporations.

— Dun & Bradstreet, Inc., Key Business Ratios.

— 10K report of your corporation (look at the president's statement).

— Market studies prepared for your corporation.

— Trade journal articles on your industry located through the *Business Periodical Guide* and *F&S Guide*.

- Industry experts whose opinions you should seek out include:

    — The analyst for the appropriate industry from the Bureau of Industrial Economics, Department of Commerce, Washington, D.C.

    — The trade association staff for your industry's trade association.

    — Market analysts for your industry (ask a reference librarian at a business library or get names from articles in trade journals).

    — If possible, sales and production managers at your company.

    — There are benchmarking criteria available for many industries through federally funded regional technology centers, such as the NIST Manufacturing Extension Partnership (MEP) organizations mentioned above.

- Identify product lines currently and potentially available and the ability to build market share as an independent company. Sources include local management, prospective management, industry publications, and industry experts.
- Review what the capability of distribution channels will be if your entity becomes an independent company.
- Explore possible marketing relationships with the seller or others.
- Evaluate the current customer base; include a review of customers lost and gained in recent years and any information available on future prospects for your business with them and, for customers who represent a high percentage of your business, their future market prospects.
- Research industry trends, major technological changes, import threats, and the potential of the target company to compete with existing products or new products the company has the capacity to produce.
- Research the company's competitive position with respect to product lines, quality, pricing structure and burden rate.
- Assess the effect of increasing environmental regulation regarding production and use of products.
- Where possible, compare product price, quality, delivery, and market share with competition for major product lines.
- Review market conclusions with industry experts and (where present) international union representatives for a "reality check" on your projections.

Management/Human Resources

The following analysis should tell you whether you have the basic personnel necessary to run a stand-alone company and whether they can work together in the complex process required to create and operate an employee-owned company.

- Evaluate management capability and continuity in key areas, including finance, operations and marketing. A competent and impartial outsider must do this assessment. The parties, labor and management alike, generally lack objectivity on this question.

- Assess management and workforce capability and potential to reduce expenses, especially in recession or other negative circumstances. This generally requires a knowledgeable outsider who carefully listens to the parties and does independent research regarding the value of similar ideas tried at the target location and elsewhere.

- Assess the potential to fill new and replacement positions of management and skilled workers.

- Assess the potential to replace key management and support functions performed by parent company.

- Assess management and labor support for employee ownership and the capacity to work together (particularly in cases where labor/management history has been difficult).

- Assess the skills of middle management.

Operations/Manufacturing

The following items bear on whether your company is an efficient producer in its market or the market you expect to enter.

- Assess the adequacy and condition of raw materials, the availability of standard parts, and the effectiveness of inventory controls and purchasing procedures.

- Assess the effect of plant design and the level of technology on productivity (production bottlenecks), and evaluate the level and type of technology in use compared to the company's competition.

- Evaluate the company's order turnaround and lead time and its competitive position regarding delivery.

- Evaluate the operating capability of the company's machinery and physical plant.

- Evaluate productivity, efficiency, and job costing information and compare potential production capacity, in units, with current performance.

- Determine the company's burden rate and compare it with industry averages. Identify means to improve the burden rate in comparison with competition.

- Assess the effectiveness of quality control systems.
- Review cost estimating procedures and compare the cost of completed jobs to estimates. Assess the company's capability to assume estimating responsibility, particularly if its parent currently does estimating.

Financial

The following items will help you determine a reasonable price for the company, whether its costs are competitive, and whether the new entity can afford the capital investment and working capital costs necessary to survive and compete.

- Review historical financial information and obtain background information for the company's current financial condition.
- Compare the company's operating expenses, labor rate, financial performance, and cost structure with its competition and with industry norms.
- Develop a preliminary financial model, including an integrated income statement, a balance sheet, cash flow projections, and a break-even analysis.
- Determine the savings necessary to operate as a profitable employee-owned company.
- Determine the new costs (or savings) of new services to be incurred as a stand-alone operation.
- Estimate the value/purchase price, the cost of capital improvements, and working capital needs.
- Assess potential collateral coverage for securing financing.
- Assess the value of work in process.
- Estimate equity and debt the employees might raise to finance the buyout, including seller financing.
- Evaluate the strength of the investment for the employees compared with their alternatives.
- Outline prospective alternative financing options.

Legal

- Outline and evaluate options for legal structures involving a possible joint venture with the parent company or other equity investors, if appropriate.
- Outline options for the legal structure for the employee-owned entity, including ESOPs, industrial or worker cooperatives, broad stock options, S corporation, C corporation, limited liability company, etc., if a buyout seems feasible.
- Provide to the seller and financial analyst for the buyout committee information on the tax advantages available to the seller(s) and the prospective new company.
- Identify potential legal obstacles to a buyout, paying particular attention to environmental, pension, and retiree health insurance issues.
- Assess the owner's willingness to sell to employees, including the price and terms.
- Assess the effect of the competition (to the new employee-owned company) arising from the current owner's continued participation in the market or through his or her other companies or divisions, and assess ameliorating such competition with non-competition agreements.
- Assess the company's ability to develop an affordable transition structure resulting in a stable, surviving company.
- Estimate the need for future operating or subcontracting agreements.

Report

A finished prefeasibility study should conclude with a report to the buyout committee that includes an analysis of the company showing:

- Its management, manufacturing, market, financial, human resource, and legal status.
- Its competitive position and the market for its products.

- Its chief strengths and weaknesses compared to its competitors.
- The purchase price, working capital, capital expenditures, and personnel changes necessary to make it viable.
- Its approximate fair market value as-is.
- Forecasted financial statements under good, bad, and average scenarios for the next three to five years based on clearly defined sets of assumptions for each scenario.
- Likely financing options.
- A recommendation whether, given all the above data, there are one or more realistic employee ownership options it is worthwhile to pursue.

The Full Feasibility Study: A Checklist

A feasibility study will differ greatly depending on the type of company and its circumstances. The purpose of the following discussion is not to describe how to do a feasibility study. The specific steps vary significantly from case to case, and the employees certainly do not need to be able to perform the analyses. Nevertheless, they do need to be concerned about whether the final product they receive as a feasibility study deals with the relevant issues, and they need to know how to interpret the results. Not every item on the list below will apply to every situation. It is offered as an aid for a buyout committee to use as a basis for creating a contract with its consultants. There are four basic parts to the feasibility study:

1. Market factors—the demand for the product.
2. Plant factors—the viability of the plant with a small investment.
3. Financial factors.
4. Financing and transaction structuring.

The following sections describe the relevant points the consultant should investigate and the results that employees should seek. It may be desirable to have a contract with a consultant that requires the following analyses:

1. **Market Factors**
    a. *Future Market for Each Product*
        __ Short-term and long-term demand outlook
        __ New uses for your products
        __ New substitutes for your products
        __ New, potentially profitable, product lines
        __ New competition from abroad
        __ If your product is an input for another product, short-term and long-term outlook for industry using your product
        __ Your market share by product line
        __ Shifts in your market share
        __ If the market is changing, niches for your product

        Results sought: whether you can expect continued demand for your products and, if so, approximately how many units you can expect to sell.

    b. *Concentration/Competition in the Industry*
        __ Type of market (local, regional, or national)
        __ Number or changes in number (new plants, plant closures) of companies in market
        __ Names of dominant producers and estimates of their market shares
        __ Changes in imports
        __ New production technologies; whether your plant has them and their importance
        __ Integration of your facility relative to competitors
        __ Distance from markets relative to competitors

        Results sought: Whether your company has any unique advantages or disadvantages relative to competitors.

The Feasibility Study for the Employee-Led Buyout

c. **Feasibility of Competition by a New Entity**

   (1) Basis of competition for customers in your industry
   - __ Importance of brand name
   - __ Number of brands
   - __ Homogeneity of product
   - __ Effectiveness of price cutting
   - __ Whether existing company is a major brand
   - __ How existing company has competed

   Results sought: Whether the employee-owned company will be able to compete for customers.

   (2) Normal Industry Distribution Channels
   - __ Do most companies in industry use factory direct sales, distributors, or manufacturers' representatives?
   - __ What channels has existing management used?
   - __ What distribution facilities (e.g., warehouses) will the employee-owned company need, and are they available?
   - __ Can the company keep its existing distribution channels and contacts? If not, are there channels it could easily adopt?
   - __ Will the company need to obtain a large new sales force?
   - __ Are customers willing to purchase goods from the new employee-owned company?
   - __ Are any large customers willing to provide letters of intent to purchase from the new company?

   Results sought: Whether there is a means of distribution available to the employee-owned company that will not require a new, complex network.

(3) Sources of Inputs at Competitive Prices

__ What are the current suppliers of inputs (raw materials, etc.)?

__ What are the potential new sources of inputs?

__ Do current suppliers serve other facilities owned by your corporation?

__ Will the employee-owned company purchase a sufficient amount of inputs to command competitive prices?

__ Are there any very large suppliers of inputs?

__ Are any large suppliers willing to provide letters of intent to sell to the new facility?

Results sought: Whether the employee-owned facility can expect to have reliable sources of supply at a competitive price.

2. Plant Factors

a. Physical Condition of Plant and Equipment

__ Historical maintenance schedule and changes in maintenance

__ Historical reinvestment plan and changes in plan

__ Average age of major capital equipment and remaining useful life of equipment

__ Age of facility relative to average age for other plants owned by parent company and by other companies

__ Need for major capital expenditures for maintenance, modernization, and/or regulation compliance

__ Estimated value of plant and equipment to be purchased[6]

Results sought: Whether the facility has been maintained enough to allow continued productive use. Whether large capital expenditures can be avoided, at least in the first three to five years, or if needed within that time can pay for themselves. Which of the facilities for sale are needed by the employee-owned company, and what their maximum value to the new company will be.

b. **Organizational Structure: Leadership, Functions, and Facilities**
   - __ Whether the facility is a profit center or a cost center
   - __ Functions that would be included in a purchase of the facility, including personnel, marketing, sales, finance, and general management
   - __ Personnel needed to fill gaps in functions
   - __ Whether the facilities at the plant are complete or additional facilities would be required, such as warehouses
   - __ Ability to keep top and middle management on board, if capable, or attract new, experienced management
   - __ Whether the existing work force has the necessary skills to operate the employee-owned facility and is willing to do so
   - __ Products or services transferred from other plants
   - __ Products transferred to other plants

   Results sought: Whether the employee-owned company can have a smooth transition. This is determined by whether it can function as an independent facility without needing to be reorganized, whether it can be separated from current ownership without losing key suppliers or markets, and whether it can depend on having a committed management to lead it.

c. **Plant Strengths and Weaknesses (based on the previous market and cost analyses)**
   - __ Reputation of the facility, including whether it has long-term suppliers and customers, and what their satisfaction with the facility is.
   - __ Willingness of suppliers and customers to deal with the new company

- Quality or efficiency as a producer relative to other producers
- Low or high cost producer in its industry for each product
- Uniqueness of product offerings
- Other strengths and weaknesses

Results sought: Whether the facility has the goodwill of its suppliers and customers, whether these suppliers and customers will deal with the new company, and whether its competitiveness with other facilities is enhanced or reduced due to specific strengths or weaknesses.

3. Financial Factors

a. Economics of the Plant/Company

(1) Cost structure for last three to five years for each product line, including costs of materials, labor, energy, maintenance, allocated overhead, and number of units of output.
   - Whether any unit costs are assessed at transfer prices (if so, revalue them to market prices)
   - Changes over time in the shares of costs and reasons
   - Changes over time in the usage of any input and reasons
   - Historical capacity use and efficient use levels

(2) Operating margins, computed using historical prices and costs
   - Trend in prices and reasons for that trend
   - Product lines with largest margins
   - Adjustments to mix that would increase plant margins

(3) Break-Even Volume
   - Minimum volume of output at which revenues equal costs

- Volume of output that maximizes profit margin
- Implications of optimal output for necessary changes in current output and employment for employee-owned company
- Feasibility of being able to sell optimal output given market projections about size of total market

(4) Profitability, computed from earnings data for facility for last five years or by subtracting from operating margins, unallocated fixed costs, estimated corporate charges, current interest costs, and depreciation expenses

- Trends in profitability
- How changes in mix identified above would change profits

(5) Cash flow for the last five years, using the data above on profits (after tax computations), adding back depreciation expenses and subtracting out changes in working capital, department repayment, and capital expenditures.

- Whether cash flow provided by operations has been sufficient to support necessary expenditures (compare profit plus depreciation to capital expenditures and debt repayment)
- If there are costs hanging over the plant for deferred maintenance, deferred replacement, pension or retiree health insurance or regulatory compliance, has plant cash flow been sufficient to finance them? If not, how much outside capital would be needed to finance them?
- If the prospective buyout target has been an independent business, additions to debt or equity capital in the last five years
- Whether any of the facility's assets are secured by debt

Results sought: Whether the facility has historically shown economic viability, including whether it has been able to control its costs and maintain profit margins, whether it has operated at optimal levels of output and with an optimal mix of its products, whether the new worker-owned company could expect a market for the volume of output at which it breaks even and for the volume of output at which it maximizes profit, whether it has been able to finance through internal cash flow its own working capital and at least some of its other capital needs, and whether it has been able to raise any outside capital in the past. For all of the above, the reasons why the company did or did not achieve these profit, output, and financing aims.

b. *Feasibility of Improving Operating Margins, Profitability, and Cash Flow*

   (1) Ability to Control Costs

   __ Cost reductions that could be made and their effect on profit margins; in particular, the feasibility of reducing overhead, improving inventory control, reducing spoilage and waste, reducing absenteeism, finding cheaper suppliers. The willingness of employees to trade off ownership for wage reductions (level of deferrals they are willing to consider); generally it is not advisable to trade the pension plan for ownership of the company.

   (2) Ability to Change Mix and Level of Output

   __ Change in mix that would raise overall profits

   __ Changes in output that are within the limits of the market that would raise overall profits

   (3) Ability to Raise Prices

   __ Based on the market study, is it possible to raise prices and roughly by how much?

   (4) Ability to Introduce New Products

   __ What are compatible new products? (See the market study)

- Operating margins on these products versus existing products

Results sought: Whether profits can be increased by moderate cost reductions, changes in mix, changes in level of output, the introduction of new products, or price increases.

c. **How Economics Would Change for the Employee-Owned Facility**

(1) Analyze the effect on profitability and cash flow of:

- Feasible changes in costs, prices, product mix, and products investigated above
- Different levels of capacity usage
- Required replacement of management staff and/or corporate functions
- Training costs for new employees
- Lower wages
- Initiating new sources of supply and/or customers
- Making deferred replacement, maintenance, and modernization expenditures

(2) Estimate future operating margins, profits, and streams of cash flows for three years, taking into account the effects of the changes in (1) immediately above.

(3) Compute working capital needs. If there is no good basis to estimate working capital needs, an approximation would be total operating expenses for four months (including rent, inventory, wages, leasehold improvements, and known interest costs) plus reserve to carry accounts receivable plus petty cash.

(4) Estimate costs of purchasing necessary facilities from existing owners or others (see "Plant Factors"). Also estimate financing costs based upon your expectations as to sources of financing and potential cost (see "Financing" section).

(5) Compare the estimated cash flows to the sum of the costs estimated in (3) and (4) using net present value analysis.[7] This must be repeated once financing costs are more exactly estimated.

Results sought: Whether the employee-owned company can achieve a rate of return high enough to maintain an efficient facility, pay back its lenders, and repay the employees for their investment.

4. Financing/Transaction Structuring Factors

Before financing can be sought, some assumptions must be made about security design, equity allocation, and corporate and ESOP governance. The consultant should discuss with the buyout group their desires and the importance of each to them. The buyout group may have little leverage over these matters. Investors and lenders often dictate these terms. However, a discussion with the consultant about the various options in these areas before he or she seeks investors gives the buyout group its best opportunity to affect the outcome.

Securities design refers to the types of stock, bonds, warrants, and so on that each party would get in the transaction. *Equity allocation* between investors is the allocation of common and preferred stock between all the parties, particularly the ESOP, management, and outside investors. *Corporate and ESOP governance* covers all the questions about who votes on what matters within the corporation, how the stock in the ESOP is to be voted, how the ESOP trustee is selected, and the ESOP trustee's powers.

Evaluating the Feasibility Study

Once the results of the feasibility study are obtained, the employees must decide whether to proceed with the proposed employee buyout. Where the results concerning market factors, plant factors, and potential improvement in these factors are overwhelmingly negative or positive, the decision may be easy. Because this will generally not be the case, it will probably be necessary to weigh the results carefully, considering the difficulties posed by each problem. The questions in the next section will be of some help in this task (other sources of advice include the consultant who prepared the feasibility study and potential investors in the company). These questions should be answered in the course of the feasibility study.

For an employee buyout to be advisable, either (1) the answers to all of the "market" and "plant" questions below should be affirmative, or (2) the answers to all of the "market" questions should be affirmative, and any answers to "plant" questions that are negative should be canceled by positive options under "potential improvements."

The "financial factors" help determine if the target company can withstand the debt load that the transaction would place upon it.

The "financing/transaction structuring" issues must be addressed to determine whether the buyout group is willing to go forward with a transaction structured in the fashion the investment banker believes is most likely to be required by the equity sources.

Of course, there will be situations in which a decision is made to proceed when these preconditions are not met. The employees in these cases must present to investors and themselves convincing reasons why the new company will succeed. The document used to convince investors to participate in the buyout is the business plan.

1. Market Factors

a. Can you expect continued demand for your products and, if so, approximately how many units can you expect to sell?
Yes ___   No ___   Number ___

b. Is it likely that your company will be able to compete for customers?
Yes ___   No ___

c. Is there a means of distribution available to your company that can be put into place in time to ensure uninterrupted distribution?
Yes ___   No ___

d. Can your company expect to have reliable sources of supplies at a competitive price?
Yes ___   No ___

2. Plant Factors

a. Has the facility been maintained enough to allow continued productive use? Can large capital expenditures be avoided in the next few years?
Yes____   No____

b. Does your company have, or can it obtain, necessary staff and facilities to function independently as soon as a transition is made to a worker-owned company?
Yes____   No____

c. Can your company retain current key suppliers and markets?
Yes____   No____

d. Does your company have, and can it continue to keep, the goodwill of its suppliers and customers?
Yes____   No____

e. Does your company have a committed management to lead it?
Yes____   No____

f. Has your company historically earned a profit? If not, was it due to causes that can be reversed?
Yes____   No____

g. Would your company break even given expected sales volume from the "Market Factors" section above?
Yes____   No____

h. Can your company expect to be able to finance its own working capital and some part of its other capital needs after one year of operation?
Yes____   No____

3. **Potential Improvements**

    a. If your company historically has not earned a profit, can profits be improved through moderate cost reductions or price increases?

    Yes____ No____

    b. Can profits be improved through changing levels of the output or the mix of products, or introducing new products?

    Yes____ No____

    c. Can profits be improved through taking better advantage of unique characteristics of your companies?

    Yes____ No____

    d. Can your company achieve a rate of return sufficient to maintain an efficient facility, repay its lenders, and repay employees and investors for their investment?

    Yes____ No____

4. **Financial Factors**

    a. Can the new company survive with the new debt a leveraged buyout would place on it?

    Yes____ No____

    b. Can the new company get sufficient working capital to see it through a series of rough times?

    Yes____ No____

5. **Financing/Transaction Structuring**

    a. Can the buyout committee live with the proposed equity design?

    Yes____ No____

b. Can the buyout committee live with the proposed equity allocation?

   Yes___   No___

c. Does the buyout committee agree with the consultant on a corporate and ESOP governance structure that the investment banker is willing to try to finance?

   Yes___   No___

Conclusion

A feasibility study attempts to provide an accurate picture of the company as it currently exists and to project what it will look like over the next three to five years (and occasionally longer if so required), based on a set of assumptions concerning ownership, markets, financing, products, costs of production, etc. As the buyer group, you must clearly think through everything you know about the company and what you desire from the buyout before you commission a feasibility study. You must make clear to the consultant you hire what you want to find out and what your desires are. You should provide your consultant with all the information on the company that you can obtain. You should hire someone who has experience not only in doing such studies but also in getting the resulting transactions implemented and financed. You should ask your consultant whether he or she thinks you are asking all the necessary questions and whether he or she sees other important questions that need answering.

To get the most benefit from your study, you must be an active participant in determining the questions asked and in analyzing the answers provided. Your contract with the consultant should lay out in writing the questions you wish to have answered. If, upon receiving the feasibility study report, you feel questions you sought answers to were not answered, raise those questions with your consultant. You may not be an expert in financial analysis, but you do know quite a lot about the company for which you work. Use your common sense and collective knowledge as a guide throughout the process. The more you take charge of the process, the more likely you are to be satisfied with the result.

Notes

1. Part of this chapter is based on the State of Michigan prefeasibility study guidelines designed by James Houck of the Michigan Jobs Commission. The author would also like to specially thank Andrew Torgove for his assistance in reviewing and suggesting revisions to this chapter based on his experience in performing feasibility studies in both the private and public sectors. Andrew Torgove is a senior associate with the investment banking firm of Houlihan Lokey Howard & Zukin, which specializes in ESOP transactions.
2. A "leveraged" buyout is a purchase of a company in which most or all of the purchase price and working capital is borrowed.
3. A "confidentiality agreement" is a contract between the seller and the buyer and/or any of the buyer's consultants, business partners or lenders, promising not to use the information provided for any purpose other than to evaluate the potential purchase of the business. It is not to be used for any competitive or collective bargaining purposes, etc.
4. "Due diligence" is intensive legal, accounting, real estate, and environmental research performed by buyers and lenders before closing a transaction to make certain they know what they are buying and the liabilities included in it. This investigation tests many of the assumptions of the initial information that was used for the letter of intent.
5. A "letter of intent" is a letter from the prospective buyer to the prospective seller outlining a transaction generally, and offering to purchase at a given price, assuming certain facts prove to be true. It is usually only a few pages long, and is based on whatever information the seller has provided. That information is assumed to be correct for the purpose of the letter of intent offer. It is later tested in the due diligence phase of the transaction.
6. A well-qualified appraiser of assets may be needed for this analysis. The appraisal will cover land, buildings, inventory, and equipment that will be useful for the new company. The business is worth the market value of its assets that are necessary to conduct business plus a premium if the business is especially profitable or minus a discount if it is unprofitable.
7. A "net present value analysis" allows you to compare income you receive in the future to cash you pay out now to buy the plant. It takes into account the fact that both inflation and the ability to invest money now and earn a return rather than spending it reduce the value of income received in the future.

Chapter 9

ESOPs in Mergers and Acquisitions

Laurence A. Goldberg

During the last several years, closely held companies have experienced a high rate of consolidation through mergers and acquisitions. Many closely held companies view acquisitions as one of the most important components of their strategic planning for the future. To gain a competitive edge in the corporate acquisitions marketplace, some ESOP-owned companies have structured acquisitions so as to provide the tax-deferred sale benefits of Section 1042 of the Internal Revenue Code of 1986, as amended (the "Code") to the shareholders of the company to be acquired.

This chapter describes the Section 1042 tax benefit and explains some of the acquisition structures that ESOP-owned companies may use to allow a corporate acquisition transaction to be combined with a tax-deferred sale of stock to an ESOP by the shareholders of the company to be acquired. The term "Acquirer" will refer to the ESOP-owned company that wishes to complete a corporate acquisition, and the term "Target" will refer to the company to be acquired.

The Section 1042 Tax Benefit

A shareholder in a closely held company who sells all or a portion of his or her stock to an ESOP may defer or avoid incurring federal capital gains tax on the sale if the transaction qualifies under Section 1042 of the Code. Section 1042 requires that the seller reinvest the sales proceeds in certain "qualified replacement property" (QRP), which Section 1042(c)(4) defines as securities (stocks, bonds, etc.) of U.S. operating companies. So, for example, securities issued by government entities or foreign corporations, or passive investment instruments such as mutual funds, would not qualify as QRP. Immediately after the ESOP purchases stock from the seller, the ESOP must own at least 30% of each class of stock of the company or 30% of the total value of all stock of the company (excluding non-convertible, non-voting preferred stock) on a fully diluted basis. The stock sold to the ESOP must have been owned by the seller for at least three years before the sale to the ESOP (the usual tax rules, including carryover basis rules, apply in determining the holding period).

The seller must sell to the ESOP stock that meets the requirements of Section 409(l) of the Code, which requires either common stock (with a combination of the best dividend and voting rights) or preferred stock convertible into such common stock.

Impact on Target Purchase Price

The total tax deferral to be realized by the shareholder of Target under Section 1042 represents the potential adjustment to the purchase price Acquirer would otherwise pay to purchase Target. Assume that Target has a fair sale value of $10 million and that for income tax purposes the shareholder of Target has a zero basis in his or her shares of Target. A sale by the Target shareholder of his or her Target stock to Acquirer would ordinarily result in a $10 million long-term capital gain, generating total federal and state income tax of $2.5 million, if one assumes an effective combined federal and state tax rate of 25% on long-term capital gains. This potential tax savings of $2.5 million establishes a range in which Acquirer and the Target shareholder would be willing to negotiate. Acquirer would seek a purchase price reduction approaching the $2.5 million, while the Target shareholder would attempt to obtain as much of the $10 million purchase price as well as the Section 1042 tax benefit.

Under these facts, a Target shareholder should not be willing to sell for any less than $7.5 million. Moreover, since Section 1042 provides a tax deferral rather than a permanent tax elimination, the Target shareholder should consider the length of time he or she expects to defer the capital gains tax and determine a present value for the $2.5 million tax deferral. For a seller who intends to retain the QRP until death, thus permanently eliminating the capital gains tax liability, the present value of the tax deferral may approach the full $2.5 million. However, this seller should still consider the burden of the reinvestment restrictions of the QRP rules of Section 1042. For a seller who expects to need some of the cash received from the ESOP during his or her lifetime, the $2.5 million tax deferral may have a present value of less than one-half of the face amount.

Certainly, the foregoing analysis shows that Acquirer should first evaluate the total potential purchase price reduction. If the amount of this reduction is substantial, then pursuit of a transaction structure that combines the acquisition with Section 1042 is worthwhile. On the other hand, if the potential savings is relatively small, either because Target is small or the seller will not substantially benefit from the Section 1042 tax deferral, then Acquirer may find that the Section 1042 element of the transaction is not feasible due to the added costs and complexity. The shareholder of Target may find Section 1042 of limited benefit if his or her tax basis in Target stock is relatively high, if the shareholder needs to spend most of the cash he or she would receive from the ESOP (and thus could not reinvest in QRP), if the shareholder does not wish to invest in the types of assets that meet the QRP standard, or if some of the shareholder's stock does not qualify for Section 1042 treatment (e.g., such stock may have been acquired in the manner described in either Section 1042(c)(1)(B)(i) or (ii) of the Code).

Considerations in Structuring the Transaction

The Easy Way Does Not Work

The shareholders of Target cannot simply sell their Target stock to Acquirer's ESOP and qualify for Section 1042 treatment. At the time of such sale, Target and Acquirer are unrelated companies and therefore not in the same "controlled group of corporations" within the meaning of Section 409(l)(4) of the Code. Therefore, the stock of Target does not constitute "qualified securities" within the meaning of Section 1042(c)(1) of the Code with respect to an ESOP maintained by Acquirer. (The stock of Target could constitute "qualified securities" with respect to an ESOP maintained by Target.) For the transaction to work properly, the shareholder of Target must first obtain stock that will constitute "qualified securities" in exchange for his or her Target stock. Alternatively, Target could establish its own ESOP and the shareholder of Target could sell his or her Target stock to the Target ESOP. This technique is described further below.

The Target Shareholder Needs Acquirer's Stock

In order to place qualified securities into the seller's hands, Target and Acquirer may engage in a tax-free reorganization of the two companies, resulting in the Target shareholder exchanging his or her Target stock for Acquirer's stock on a tax-free basis. The owner of Target would give up his or her stock in Target in exchange for stock of Acquirer. Therefore, this reorganization results in: (1) Acquirer obtaining control of Target (which is Acquirer's primary objective) and (2) the former shareholder of Target becoming the owner of Acquirer stock on a tax-free basis. Then the ESOP stock purchase can proceed. However, it is critical that the reorganization be accomplished on a tax-free basis. Otherwise, the exchange of Target stock for Acquirer stock would itself be taxable to the seller, causing the seller to incur capital gains tax on the exchange of the stock. Any subsequent sale of the stock to the ESOP would not provide the expected benefits of Section 1042 because the seller would have to recognize the taxable gain on the prior exchange, rendering the Section 1042 election valueless to the seller.

Conflict Between Sections 368 and 1042 of the Code

A desire to complete a prearranged sale of Acquirer stock by the Target shareholder immediately following the reorganization may conflict with certain requirements under the tax-free reorganization provisions of Section 368(a) of the Code and related regulations. Therefore, the reorganization must be designed in a manner that will permit its tax-free nature to survive the subsequent sale of Acquirer stock by the former shareholder of Target. Section 368 of the Code and related regulations set forth the conditions which must be met in order for such transactions to be treated as tax-free reorganizations. Therefore, the restructuring of Target and Acquirer must be designed to comply with the requirements of Section 368(a) of the Code.

The Section 368 Requirements

Section 368(a) of the Code describes several types of reorganizations that can qualify as tax-free. The two types of reorganizations most relevant to a Section 1042 transaction are the "A Reorganization" described in Section 368(a)(1)(A) and the "B Reorganization" described in Section 368(a)(1)(B). (A version of the A Reorganization, known as a "triangular merger," also will be considered.) These two types of reorganizations are briefly described below.

A Reorganization An A Reorganization is a statutory merger of two corporations. Target could merge into Acquirer and cease to exist after the merger. The Target shareholder would receive stock in Acquirer in exchange for the shareholder's Target stock.

An alternative would be for Acquirer to create a wholly owned subsidiary (an "Acquisition Sub") and then merge the Acquisition Sub and Target. The Target shareholder receives stock in Acquirer, and Target becomes a wholly owned subsidiary of Acquirer. If the Acquisition Sub survives the merger, it is known as a forward triangular merger, and if the Target survives, it is known as a reverse triangular merger. In either case, Target ultimately becomes a wholly owned subsidiary of Acquirer, and the shareholder of Target becomes a shareholder of Acquirer. The Target shareholder may receive only stock in Acquirer in exchange for his or her Target stock, or the shareholder may receive a combination of Acquirer's stock and cash.

B Reorganization A B Reorganization involves the acquisition of "control" of Target (as defined below) by Acquirer in exchange solely for the voting stock of Acquirer. In this reorganization, Target becomes a subsidiary of Acquirer, and the Target shareholder receives stock of Acquirer.

For purposes of combining a tax-free reorganization with a Section 1042 transaction, two of the requirements under Section 368 (a) of the Code (and the related regulations) merit special consideration: "continuity of interest" and control.

Continuity of Interest In both the A and the B Reorganizations, the pre-1998 Section 368 regulations (and case law) required the shareholder of Target to retain a continuing equity interest in the business the shareholder had transferred to Acquirer. This requirement is generally referred to as the "Continuity of Interest" (COI) test. COI is met by having the shareholder of Target receive stock in Acquirer rather than cash. In a B Reorganization, the shareholders of Target are only permitted to receive voting stock of Acquirer. In an A Reorganization, it is generally permissible for the Target shareholder to receive 50% to 60% of the sales price in the form of Acquirer's stock and still meet the standard of preserving a continuing equity interest. The Internal Revenue Service (IRS) takes the position that without a continuing equity interest, the shareholder has simply sold Target for cash to Acquirer and the sale should be a taxable transaction. Where the seller retains a continuing equity interest, the Code treats the transaction as a mere reorganization of ownership interest which does not trigger taxation.

Under the pre-1998 regulations, the COI requirement meant that a purported tax-free merger could be treated as a taxable merger if it were followed immediately by a prearranged sale of Acquirer's stock to an ESOP by the Target shareholder.

Control Test In both the A and the B Reorganization, the Code requires that Acquirer obtain "control" of Target, with control defined in Section 368(c) to mean at least 80% of the total combined voting power and at least 80% of the total number of shares of all other classes of stock of the Target.

Transaction Structures Used Before 1998 COI Regulations

Before the promulgation of the 1998 amendments to Treas. Reg. § 1.368-1(e) (the "1998 COI Regulations") described below, several transaction structures were used in an effort to permit the shareholder of Target to sell to the Acquirer's ESOP in connection with the acquisition. The following are four of the more common techniques used before the 1998 COI Regulations:

Reverse Acquisition

The parties would combine Acquirer and Target through a tax-free reorganization under Section 368(a) of the Code, in which Acquirer would merge into Target, with Target being the surviving corporation. Target would assume the ESOP of Acquirer. Under the COI rules, the shareholder of Target could then sell his or her Target stock immediately to what became the Target ESOP without violating the COI requirement. The COI rules look to continuity of ownership among the shareholders of the acquired company and ignore continuity of interest with respect to ownership of the acquiring entity. Assuming the former shareholders of Acquirer do not immediately sell the Target stock they receive in the merger, COI is met. Similarly, transactions have sometimes been structured as a "reverse" B Reorganization, followed by the Section 1042 sale. In a reverse B Reorganization, Target issues its stock to the shareholders of Acquirer in exchange for Acquirer stock, resulting in Acquirer becoming a wholly owned subsidiary of Target. Although the original shareholder of Target would then sell immediately to the ESOP, COI is met because the "acquired" company's shareholder is not a seller and retains a continuing equity interest in the business.

Some companies have found it difficult to use this reverse acquisition technique because the Acquirer either ceases to exist or becomes a wholly owned subsidiary of another company. In particular, companies that operate under state licensing rules, such as construction contractors, may find the loss of a valuable license could prevent the use of the reverse acquisition technique. Certainly, other companies have been uncomfortable with losing the company's traditional corporate existence as a "cost" of completing a corporate acquisition.

Dual ESOPs

Target would establish its own ESOP. The shareholder of Target would then sell all of his or her Target stock to Target's ESOP. Acquirer would participate by guaranteeing the bank financing required by the Target ESOP. Immediately after the transaction, the Target ESOP would merge into the Acquirer ESOP. At that time, Acquirer's ESOP would own 100% of the stock of Target and would retain its pre-transaction ownership position in Acquirer. In order to comply with the COI rules, Target and Acquirer would continue to be maintained as separate corporations for one to three years. At a future date, Target would be merged into Acquirer, with the Acquirer ESOP exchanging its Target stock for additional stock in Acquirer.

In Technical Advice Memoranda 9631002 (September 26, 1995), 9631003 (September 26, 1995), and 9705004 (December 15, 1996), the IRS agreed that the "dual ESOP" transaction structure would not cause a violation of the qualified plan rules under Section 401(a) of the Code. In addition, the IRS agreed that the sellers were entitled to Section 1042 treatment on the sale of their shares to a transitory ESOP. However, the facts of the TAM appear to imply that the corporate merger of Target and Acquirer could occur shortly after the merger ESOP, without regard to the COI rules. The unique facts in that situation (some of which are not described in the TAM) supported the subsequent corporate merger. Moreover, the three TAMs do not address the qualification of the corporate reorganization under Section 368(a) of the Code.

Holding Company

This transaction structure turns on the Section 351 tax-free incorporation rules rather than the Section 368 reorganization rules. The shareholders of Acquirer and Target would establish a holding company ("Newco") tax-free under Section 351 of the Code as a first step, and exchange their stock in Acquirer and Target, respectively, for Newco stock. Acquirer and Target would become wholly owned subsidiaries of Newco. The Acquirer ESOP would be assumed by Newco. The former shareholder of Target would then sell his or her Newco stock to an ESOP delivering Section 1042 treatment.

Section 351(a) of the Code does not include a COI requirement. However, Section 351 requires that the shareholders of Target and Acquirer who create Newco must obtain "control" of Newco within the meaning of Section 368(c) of the Code (the 80% test described above). The Treasury Regulations promulgated under Section 351 of the Code provide that the control test will fail to be met if a prearranged sale of stock by one of the transferors to Newco causes the original group of Newco shareholders to own less than 80% of the stock under Section 368(c) of the Code. However, the IRS has ruled that shares of Newco stock transferred from one shareholder to another shareholder in connection with the incorporation of Newco will still be counted towards the 80% control test. Therefore, Newco's ESOP (formerly maintained by Acquirer) may purchase Newco stock from other Newco shareholders without causing the incorporation to fail the 80% control test.

Leap of Faith

From time to time, Target shareholders have agreed to exchange their Target stock for Acquirer stock in a tax-free merger, with no written assurance as to if or when their Acquirer stock might be purchased for cash by the Acquirer's ESOP. Then, one to three years following the merger, Acquirer's ESOP would offer to buy the Acquirer stock owned by Target shareholders. The parties to the transaction would conclude that because the Target shareholders were holding

Acquirer's stock for one to three years, the IRS would not treat the merger and the subsequent ESOP purchase as a single transaction. Therefore, COI would be met, and the sale to the ESOP would qualify under Section 1042. Many shareholders who want to sell Target stock for cash would not be satisfied with a transaction that does not include a written commitment on the part of Acquirer or its ESOP to purchase the Acquirer stock in the future. For this reason, probably few acquisitions have been structured in this manner.

Impact of 1998 COI Regulations

The final IRS regulations published in January 1998 under Section 368 of the Code greatly relax the COI requirements. The 1998 COI Regulations put the focus of the "continuity" requirement on the type of consideration received in the transaction by the seller rather than on the duration of the seller's retention of the consideration. The 1998 COI Regulations look to whether a proprietary interest in Target has been preserved but not to whether the former shareholders of the Target retain the equity interest.

Merger and Prearranged Sale

Under Treas. Reg. § 1.368-1(e), the following two-step transaction could be completed on a single day: Acquirer can acquire Target by merging Target into Acquirer and issuing Acquirer stock to the shareholder of Target. Then, pursuant to a prearranged, binding sales contract, the former shareholder of Target may sell his Acquirer stock to any person other than a "related person" (as defined in Treas. Reg. § 1.368-1(e)(3)). The 1998 COI Regulations would not hold the merger to be taxable even though the shareholder of Target does not personally retain any continuing interest in Acquirer.

Related Person

As noted above, the 1998 COI Regulations prohibit the Target shareholder from selling his or her Acquirer stock immediately after the merger if the purchaser is a "related person" with respect to the Acquirer. The 1998 COI Regulations provide that a "related person" is a corporation which is in the affiliated group of Acquirer under Section 1504 of the Code (the consolidated tax return rules) or is a related corporation under Section 304(a)(2) of the Code. Because these two definitions of "related person" are both limited to corporate entities, it would appear that an ESOP would not be a related person. Under this interpretation of the 1998 COI Regulations, Acquirer and Target could complete both the corporate merger and the Section 1042 transaction on the same day.

Facts and Circumstances Standard

Treas. Reg. § 1.368-1(e)(1) states that the IRS will look to "all facts and circumstances" to determine whether a proprietary interest in the Target has been preserved, as required by the regulations. A purchase of Acquirer's stock by the ESOP from former Target shareholders could be treated as analogous to a prohibited redemption of such stock by Acquirer. On one hand, the non-ESOP shareholders maintain their relative equity positions, just as in a redemption. However, this analysis would require the IRS to treat the ESOP shareholder as having no substance. This position would be in direct conflict with the requirements of Title I of the Employee Retirement Income Security Act of 1974, as amended (ERISA) which require the trustees of the ESOP to act in the best interest of ESOP participants and not merely at the direction of the corporation or other shareholders.

Step Transaction

A series of separate steps taken by a taxpayer may be treated by the IRS as a single transaction under a judicially created doctrine known as the "step transaction" doctrine. By collapsing the separate steps into a single transaction, the IRS would then recharacterize the transaction, typically in a manner that prevents the taxpayer from achieving his or her tax objective. Courts have formulated at least three different ways of applying the step transaction doctrine, although all seem to have in common the concept that separate steps which have no independent economic significance will be treated as a single transaction. It is possible the IRS could treat a stock-for-stock exchange (either an A or B Reorganization) followed immediately by a Section 1042 transaction as a single transaction. Under such an approach, the IRS might argue that the shareholder of Target effectively sold his or her Target stock in the exchange to Acquirer, and that Acquirer then sold the stock to its own ESOP. However, such an approach might require the IRS to argue that anytime a shareholder sells to an ESOP, the corporation could have achieved the same result by redeeming the shareholder's stock and then selling the shares to the company's ESOP—a result that is clearly contrary to the intent of Section 1042 of the Code.

An Alternative Approach

A recent private letter ruling issued by the IRS, PLR 200052023, provides guidance that ESOP companies may use in completing future acquisitions of other companies on a tax-favored basis. The acquisition structure used in the PLR solves a number of concerns faced in these acquisitions. In the PLR, the target company ("Target") established an ESOP ("Target ESOP") and the owners of Target sold their stock to the Target ESOP. The Target shareholders elected tax-deferred sale treatment under Section 1042 of the Code for this transaction. The Target ESOP then merged into the Acquirer's ESOP, with the result that both Acquirer and Target were owned by the Acquirer ESOP. As a final step, Acquirer then acquired all of the stock of Target from the Acquirer ESOP in a tax-free exchange. This final step caused Target to become a subsidiary of Acquirer and was intended to be a tax-free "B" reorganization.

The IRS ruled that the final step in the transaction would be treated as a tax-free "B" reorganization, that neither Acquirer nor its ESOP would have gain or loss on the exchange, and that no excise tax under Section 4978 would be incurred. The taxpayer did not ask, and the IRS did not specifically rule, that the first step, the ESOP's purchase of Target, would qualify for tax-deferred sale treatment under Section 1042 of the Code. However, the substance of the PLR appears to allow an inference that the IRS would not disallow the benefits of Section 1042 treatment.

Although the PLR is useful, the transaction described is relatively complicated. ESOP companies would find this acquisition technique worthwhile only if the size of the tax savings available to the Target shareholders was significant. Moreover, a PLR is only authority for the taxpayer to whom it is issued, and any other taxpayer must consider whether to obtain their own PLR for a transaction.

Future Transactions

The 1998 COI Regulations may provide a much-improved method for combining a corporate acquisition with a Section 1042 transaction. However, the IRS has not clarified its position with respect to some of the risks identified above in any published rulings. In 1999, the IRS informally indicated that it might conclude in connection with several pending private letter ruling requests that, under certain circumstances, an ESOP might be treated as a "related person" under the 1998 COI Regulations. However, no private letter ruling or other IRS guidance has been issued to date. Therefore, parties to these transactions may consider using one of the transaction structures in use before the issuance of the 1998 COI Regulations in order to decrease the risk associated with a particular transaction.

Alternatively, parties whose transactions can be designed to fit within the structure of PLR 200052023 (discussed above under "An Alternative Approach") may wish to use that approach to avoid the issues that arise under the 1998 COI regulations.

Conclusion

Many ESOP-owned companies have used the acquisition techniques described in this chapter to gain a competitive advantage in their corporate acquisition strategy. With the publication of final amendments to the IRS tax-free reorganization regulations, it may be possible to complete these acquisitions using greatly simplified transaction structures.

About the Authors

Laurence A. Goldberg is a partner in the San Francisco office of the law firm Kirkpatrick & Lockhart LLP. He focuses his practice on the design, implementation, and operation of ESOPs and also advises clients on various types of pension and profit sharing plans.

Luis Granados is a partner in McDermott, Will & Emery's Washington, D.C., office. He focuses his practice on ESOPs, having been active in the field for many years, and has written many articles on the subject.

David C. Light is a managing director at Duff & Phelps LLC. Mr. Light has managed a wide variety of corporate finance transactions and advisory engagements for public and private company owners, boards of directors, and trustees. His work has focused on structuring ESOP transactions, fairness opinion work for boards of directors and ESOP trustees, incentive program design, compliance work, corporate planning for owners, and litigation support. Mr. Light is president of the Business Valuation Association and is a member of the NCEO and the ESOP Association.

Richard C. May became a member of the management committee at Duff & Phelps, LLC, after its merger with Valuemetrics, a financial advisory firm he founded in 1981. He has worked with owners of privately and publicly held corporations for more than two decades, assisting in ownership succession planning and recapitalizations using debt and equity financing. He is regarded as a leading expert in business valuation, particularly ESOPs. Mr. May has served as chairman of the Valuation Advisory Committee of the ESOP Association, is a senior member of the American Society of Appraisers, is a member of the Business Valuation Association, and is an associate member of the National Center for Employee Ownership.

Robert L. McDonald is the Erwin P. Nemmers Distinguished Professor of Finance at Northwestern's Kellogg School of Management. He has been a faculty member at Northwestern since 1984 and has also served as department chair. Professor McDonald's research interests include corporate finance, taxation, derivatives, and applications of option pricing theory to corporate investments. He is co-editor of the Review of Financial Studies. Most recently, he completed an authoritative textbook, *Derivatives Markets*.

Rebecca J. Miller is a partner with the accounting firm of McGladrey & Pullen, LLP. In 1999 she was named to the U.S. Department of Labor's Advisory Council on Employee Welfare and Pension Benefit Plans. She was on the AICPA's ESOP task force responsible for drafting the current accounting standard covering ESOPs, *Statement of Position 93-6: Employers' Accounting for Employee Stock Ownership Plans*. In addition, from 1996 through 1998, Ms. Miller served on the AICPA's Employee Plans Committee, which is responsible for developing the standards covering the plan's financial reporting and the responsibilities of the plan's auditors.

Deborah Groban Olson is an attorney who has specialized since 1981 in employee ownership projects. She creates and advises employee owned companies and equity compensation plans (including ESOPs, stock options, and cooperatives), representing companies, non-profit organizations, unions, families who own companies, trusts, and employees. Olson is executive director of the Capital Ownership Group (COG), a global network and online policy institute at Kent State University, developing policy for broadening capital ownership globally. She is a board member and past board chair of the National Center for Employee Ownership (NCEO) and a board member of the European Federation of Employed Shareholders (EFES).

Scott Rodrick is the director of publications and information technology at the National Center for Employee Ownership (NCEO). Mr. Rodrick is the author of the NCEO's booklet *An Introduction to ESOPs* (6th ed. 2004), the editor and or/coauthor of various other NCEO publications, and the coeditor of *Employee Stock Ownership Plans* (Harcourt Brace, 1996, 1999). He served at the U.S. Department of Labor as an attorney-advisor before coming to the NCEO.

About the Authors

Corey Rosen is the executive director and cofounder of the National Center for Employee Ownership (NCEO). He received his Ph.D. from Cornell University in political science in 1973, taught government at Ripon College until 1976, and then served as a Senate staff member until 1981, when he cofounded the NCEO. As a Senate staffer, he helped draft some of the current ESOP legislation. Mr. Rosen has coauthored four books and written over 100 articles on various aspects of employee ownership for a variety of professional, academic, and trade publications. He has lectured on the subject across the U.S. and abroad.

Kenneth E. Serwinski is a managing director at Prairie Capital Advisors, Inc., a middle-market financial advisory firm specializing in succession planning and the implementation of exit strategies. Prairie Capital's expertise in ESOPs includes valuation, structuring financing, and managing the ESOP process.

Mary Sullivan Josephs is a senior vice president at LaSalle Bank N.A., where her group is responsible for the design, structure, and finance of ESOP transactions. Mary speaks frequently for the National Center for Employee Ownership (NCEO), the ESOP Association, and other professional associations on topics related to ESOPs, leveraged financing, and ownership succession. She is a board member of the NCEO; a member of the Economic Club of Chicago and the Chicago Finance Exchange (CFE), an organization of women executives with major financial responsibilities; and a member of the ESOP Association, where she is on the board of governors.

About the NCEO

The National Center for Employee Ownership (NCEO) is widely considered to be the leading authority in employee ownership in the U.S. and the world. Established in 1981 as a nonprofit information and membership organization, it now has roughly 3,000 members, including companies, professionals, unions, government officials, academics, and interested individuals.

The NCEO's mission is to provide the most objective, reliable information possible about employee ownership at the most affordable price possible. As part of the NCEO's commitment to providing objective information, it does not lobby or provide ongoing consulting services. The NCEO publishes a variety of materials on employee ownership and participation; its dozens of publications include many books, a newsletter for members, and the *Journal of Employee Ownership Law and Finance,* the only professional journal in the field. It holds dozens of seminars, webinars, and conferences on employee ownership annually, and it offers a variety of online courses. The NCEO's work includes extensive contacts with the media, both through articles written for trade and professional publications and through interviews with reporters. Finally, the NCEO maintains an extensive Web site at *www.nceo.org.*

Membership Benefits

NCEO members receive the following benefits:

- The bimonthly newsletter, *Employee Ownership Report,* which covers ESOPs, equity compensation, and employee participation.
- Access to the members-only area of the NCEO's Web site, which includes many resources, such as a searchable database of over 200 NCEO members who are service providers in this field, a searchable database of ESOP lenders, a searchable archive of NCEO newsletters, and legislative and regulatory updates.

- Substantial discounts on publications and events produced by the NCEO (such as this book).
- The right to telephone or email the NCEO for answers to general or specific questions regarding employee ownership.

An introductory NCEO membership costs $80 for one year ($90 outside the U.S.) and covers an entire company at all locations, a single individual offering professional services in this field, or a single individual with a business interest in employee ownership. Full-time students and faculty members who are not employed in the business sector may join at the academic rate of $35 for one year ($45 outside the U.S.).

Selected NCEO Publications

The NCEO offers a variety of publications on all aspects of employee ownership and participation. Following are descriptions of our main publications.

We publish new books and revise old ones on a yearly basis. To obtain the most current information on what we have available, visit our extensive Web site at *www.nceo.org* or call us at 510-208-1300.

Employee Stock Ownership Plans (ESOPs)

- *The ESOP Reader* is an overview of the issues involved in establishing and operating an ESOP. It covers the basics of ESOP rules, feasibility, valuation, and other matters, and then discusses managing an ESOP company, including brief case studies.

    $25 for NCEO members, $35 for nonmembers

- *Selling to an ESOP* explains how ESOPs work and then addresses legal structures, financing, and other matters, especially the tax-deferred section 1042 "rollover" that allows owners to indefinitely defer capital gains taxation on the proceeds of the ESOP sale.

    $25 for NCEO members, $35 for nonmembers

- This book, *Leveraged ESOPs and Employee Buyouts,* discusses how ESOPs borrow money to buy out entire companies, purchase shares from a retiring owner, or finance new capital. It includes detailed coverage of topics such as contribution limits.

$25 for NCEO members, $35 for nonmembers

- *S Corporation ESOPs* introduces the reader to how ESOPs work and then discusses the legal, valuation, administrative, and other issues associated with S corporation ESOPs.

  $25 for NCEO members, $35 for nonmembers

- The *Model ESOP* contains a sample ESOP plan, with alternative provisions given to tailor the plan to individual needs. It also includes a section-by-section explanation of the plan and other supporting materials.

  $50 for NCEO members, $75 for nonmembers

- *ESOP Valuation* brings together and updates where needed the best articles on ESOP valuation that we have published in our *Journal of Employee Ownership Law and Finance,* described below.

  $25 for NCEO members, $35 for nonmembers

- The *Employee Ownership Q&A Disk* gives Microsoft Windows users point-and-click access to 500 questions and answers on all aspects of ESOPs in a fully searchable hypertext format.

  $75 for NCEO members, $100 for nonmembers

- *How ESOP Companies Handle the Repurchase Obligation* includes both essays and research on the subject.

  $25 for NCEO members, $35 for nonmembers

- *The ESOP Committee Guide* describes the different types of ESOP committees, the range of goals they can address, alternative structures, member selection criteria, training, committee life cycle concerns, and other issues.

  $25 for NCEO members, $35 for nonmembers

- *Wealth and Income Consequences of Employee Ownership* reports on a study of ESOP companies in Washington State that found ESOP companies provide better benefits than other companies.

  $10 for NCEO members, $15 for nonmembers

- *ESOPs and Corporate Governance* covers everything from shareholder rights to the impact of Sarbanes-Oxley to choosing a fiduciary.

    $25 for NCEO members, $35 for nonmembers

- The *ESOP Communications Sourcebook* is a publication for ESOP companies with ideas and examples on how to communicate an ESOP to employees and market employee ownership to customers. It includes a CD with communications materials.

    $35 for NCEO members, $50 for nonmembers

Equity Compensation (Stock Options, Restricted Stock, Etc.)

- *The Stock Options Book* is a straightforward, comprehensive overview covering the legal, accounting, regulatory, and design issues involved in implementing a stock option or stock purchase plan. It is our main book on the subject.

    $25 for NCEO members, $35 for nonmembers

- *Selected Issues in Stock Options* is more detailed and specialized than *The Stock Options Book,* with chapters on issues such as administration, IPOs, and securities issues. The appendix is an exhaustive glossary of terms used in the field.

    $25 for NCEO members, $35 for nonmembers

- *Beyond Stock Options* is a guide to phantom stock, stock appreciation rights, restricted stock, direct stock purchase plans, and performance awards used as alternatives to stock options.

    $35 for NCEO members, $50 for nonmembers

- *Accounting for Equity Compensation* is a guide to the financial accounting rules that govern equity compensation programs in the United States.

    $35 for NCEO members, $50 for nonmembers

- *Tax and Securities Sources for Equity Compensation* is a compilation of statutory and regulatory material relevant to the study of equity compensation.

    $35 for NCEO members, $50 for nonmembers

About the NCEO 215

- *Equity Compensation in a Post-Expensing World* is a collection of essays on strategies for choosing and structuring equity compensation plans when expensing is required.

    $25 for NCEO members, $35 for nonmembers

- *The Employee's Guide to Stock Options* is a guide for the everyday employee that explains in an easy-to-understand format what stock is and how stock options work.

    $25 for both NCEO members and nonmembers

- *Employee Stock Purchase Plans* covers how ESPPs work, tax and legal issues, administration, accounting, communicating the plan to employees, and research on what companies are doing with their plans. The book includes sample plan documents.

    $25 for NCEO members, $35 for nonmembers

- *Model Equity Compensation Plans* provides examples of incentive stock option, nonqualified stock option, and stock purchase plans, together with brief explanations of the main documents. A disk is included with copies of the plan documents in formats any word processing program can open.

    $50 for NCEO members, $75 for nonmembers

- *Communicating Stock Options* offers practical ideas and information about how to explain stock options to employees. It includes both essays and sample communication materials.

    $35 for NCEO members, $50 for nonmembers

- *Stock Options, Corporate Performance, and Organizational Change* presents the first serious research to examine the relationship between broadly granted stock options and company performance, and the extent of employee involvement in broad option companies.

    $15 for NCEO members, $25 for nonmembers

- *Equity-Based Compensation for Multinational Corporations* describes how companies can use stock options and other equity-based programs across the world to reward a global work force. It includes a country-by-country summary of tax and legal issues.

    $25 for NCEO members, $35 for nonmembers

- *Incentive Compensation and Employee Ownership* takes a broad look at how companies can use incentives, ranging from stock plans to cash bonuses to gainsharing, to motivate and reward employees. It includes both technical discussions and case studies.

    $25 for NCEO members, $35 for nonmembers

Employee Involvement and Management

- *Ownership Management* draws upon the experience of the NCEO and of leading employee ownership companies to discuss how to build a culture of lasting innovation by combining employee ownership with employee involvement programs.

    $25 for NCEO members, $35 for nonmembers

- *Front Line Finance Facilitator's Manual* gives step-by-step instructions for teaching business literacy, emphasizing ESOPs.

    $50 for NCEO members, $75 for nonmembers

- *Front Line Finance Diskette* contains the workbook for participants in electronic form in the *Front Line Finance* course.

    $50 for NCEO members, $75 for nonmembers

- *Cultural Diversity and Employee Ownership* discusses how companies with employee stock plans deal with diversity.

    $25 for NCEO members, $35 for nonmembers

Other

- *Section 401(k) Plans and Employee Ownership* focuses on how company stock is used in 401(k) plans, both in stand-alone 401(k) plans and combination 401(k)–ESOP plans ("KSOPs").

    $25 for NCEO members, $35 for nonmembers

- *Employee Ownership Concepts in Nonprofits and Government* discusses how nonprofits and governmental units, despite their lack of stock, can implement employee ownership concepts and build a more productive and satisfying ownership culture in the workplace.

    $25 for NCEO members, $35 for nonmembers

- *Ownership Solutions* is a booklet that discusses the various ways of sharing equity with employees.

    $10 for NCEO members, $15 for nonmembers

- *Employee Ownership and Corporate Performance* reviews the research that has been done on the link between company stock plans and various aspects of corporate performance.

    $25 for NCEO members, $35 for nonmembers

- *A Conceptual Guide to Equity-Based Compensation for Non-U.S. Companies* helps companies outside the U.S. think through how to approach employee ownership.

    $25 for NCEO members, $35 for nonmembers

- *The Journal of Employee Ownership Law and Finance* is the only professional journal solely devoted to employee ownership. Articles are written by leading experts and cover ESOPs, stock options, and related subjects in depth.

    One-year subscription (four issues):
    $75 for NCEO members, $100 for nonmembers

To join the NCEO as a member or to order any of the publications listed on the preceding pages, use the order form on the following page, use the secure ordering system on our Web site at *www.nceo.org*, or call us at 510-208-1300. If you join at the same time you order publications, you will receive the members-only publication discounts.

Order Form

To order, fill out this form and mail it with your credit card information or check to the NCEO at 1736 Franklin St., 8th Flr., Oakland, CA 94612; fax it with your credit card information to the NCEO at 510-272-9510; telephone us at 510-208-1300 with your credit card in hand; or order at our Web site, *www.nceo.org*. If you are not already a member, you can join now to receive member discounts on any publications you order.

Name

Organization

Address

City, State, Zip (Country)

Telephone   Fax   E-mail

Method of Payment: ❏ Check (payable to "NCEO")   ❏ Visa   ❏ M/C   ❏ AMEX

Credit Card Number

Signature   Exp. Date

Checks are accepted only for orders from the U.S. and must be in U.S. currency.

Title	Qty.	Price	Total

Tax: California residents add 8.75% sales tax (on publications only, not membership or Journal subscriptions)

Shipping: In the U.S., first publication $5, each add'l $1; elsewhere, we charge exact shipping costs to your credit card, plus a $10 handling surcharge; no shipping charges for membership or Journal subscriptions

Introductory NCEO Membership: $80 for one year ($90 outside the U.S.)

Subtotal	$
Sales Tax	$
Shipping	$
Membership	$
TOTAL DUE	$